COMPUTERS FOR EDUCATIONAL ADMINISTRATORS

Leadership in the Information Age

COMPUTERS FOR EDUCATIONAL ADMINISTRATORS

Leadership in the Information Age

Greg Kearsley

George Washington University

ABLEX PUBLISHING CORPORATION
Norwood, New Jersey

Cover design by Thomas Phon Graphics

Library of Congress Cataloging-in-Publication Data

Kearsley, Greg, 1951–
    Computers for educational administrators: leadership in the information age / Greg Kearsley.
        p.   cm.
    Includes bibliographical references and index.
    ISBN 0-89391-649-8. — ISBN 0-89391-650-1 (pbk.)
    1. Education—Data processing.   2. Educational technology.
3. Computer managed instruction.   4. Computer-assisted instruction.
5. School management and organization—Data processing.   I. Title.
LB1028.43.K43   1990
371.2′00285—dc20   90-38885
                                                                    CIP

Ablex Publishing Corporation
355 Chestnut Street
Norwood, New Jersey 07648

Contents

PREFACE   *vii*

PROLOG   *ix*

1 • INTRODUCTION   *1*
    The school milieu   *3*
    What you need to know   *5*
    Who should read this book?   *7*
    Organization of the book   *8*
    Exercises   *9*

2 • HOW CAN COMPUTERS HELP?   *11*
    Accounting   *11*
    Attendance   *14*
    Grading   *15*
    Scheduling   *16*
    Test scoring   *17*
    Student information systems   *20*
    Other applications   *22*
    Summary   *25*
    Exercises   *26*

3 • TOOLS FOR SCHOOLS   *29*
    Word processing and desktop publishing   *29*
    Database management   *32*
    Spreadsheets   *34*
    Graphics and desktop publications   *36*
    Telecommunications   *37*
    Integrated software   *38*
    Summary   *39*
    Exercises   *40*

4 • COMPUTERS IN THE CLASSROOM   *43*
    Application programs   *43*
    Instructional software   *45*
    Programming languages   *49*
    Multimedia   *50*
    Teacher utilities and Student Management Programs   *51*
    Summary   *52*
    Exercises   *53*

**5 • EVALUATING HARDWARE
AND SOFTWARE ALTERNATIVES**   *55*
    Hardware alternatives   *55*
    Software alternatives   *61*
    Integrated Learning Systems   *67*
    Conclusions   *68*
    Exercises   *69*

6 • SUCCESSFUL COMPUTER IMPLEMENTATION   *71*
    Facilities   *71*
    Staffing   *73*
    Training   *75*
    Security   *78*
    Maintenance   *80*
    Summary   *81*
    Exercises   *82*

7 • PLANNING FOR COMPUTERS   *85*
    Identifying goals and objectives   *86*
    Acquiring hardware/software   *87*
    Implementation scheduling   *89*
    Evaluation   *93*
    Establishing policies and procedures   *95*
    Summary   *96*
    Exercises   *97*

8 • FINANCING COMPUTERS   *99*
    Cost/Benefits   *99*
    Budgeting   *102*
    Funding sources   *104*
    Expenses   *106*
    Summary   *107*
    Exercises   *108*

9 • NEW DIRECTIONS   *111*
    Networking   *111*
    Laptop computers   *115*
    Hypertext   *116*
    Artificial intelligence   *116*
    Distance learning   *119*
    Community outreach   *120*
    Summary   *123*
    Exercises   *123*

10 • WELCOME TO P.S. 1991   *127*
    Exercises   *142*

GLOSSARY   *143*

REFERENCES   *147*

APPENDIX: FURTHER RESOURCES   *151*

AUTHOR INDEX   *157*

SUBJECT INDEX   *159*

Preface

Computer technology is transforming our world. There can be no doubt that this technology will eventually transform our school system, for better or for worse. To ensure that it is for the better, we need strong leadership in the educational computing domain.

Where will this leadership come from? Will it come from computer experts? From educational researchers? Or, from computer literate teachers? It *should* come from the people who actually run our schools—principals, superintendents, department heads, deans, and board members. Educational administrators at all levels should be providing technology leadership.

This book outlines the kinds of knowledge and skills needed to assume such a leadership role. This includes knowing how computers can be used for administrative and classroom applications, how to evaluate hardware and software, and how to successfully implement computers in schools. It includes the ability to use computers in schools. It also includes the ability to use computers to improve personal productivity and the productivity of schools. Educational leaders must also be aware of emerging trends and new developments in technology for future planning.

As impressive as technology can be, it is not the answer to all problems. Computers do not address many of the social and economic issues that educational administrators face on a daily basis. What is needed is a balanced view of technology; an understanding of when and where computers can be used to advantage. This book tries to present such a perspective.

A number of individuals have provided special help in the writing of this book: Beverly Hunter, James Mecklenburger, Jane McDonald, Craig Montgomerie, and Martha Rolley. I thank them for their valuable contributions. I also want to thank the "students" who have participated in my courses on this subject; I am sure I have learned more from them than they learned from me about the challenges of using computers in education.

Greg Kearsley
Washington, DC, 1989

Prolog

Reader: Hi. I came here to learn something about the use of computers in educational administration.

Author: Well, you came to the right place. It's all here in this book.

Reader: Great! But look prof, I'm pretty busy these days...Is there some way I could just get a few questions answered and then get back to work?

Author: Hmmm. Do you know what questions you want answered?

Reader: Yeah, I've got them written down on this sheet of paper here—see?

Author: Ok, why don't you go ahead and ask your questions and I'll do my best to answer then now. Shoot.

Reader: Here's question #1: What's the best computer to buy?

Author: It doesn't really matter—buy anything.

Reader: Huh?

Author: First of all, it's the software that really matters since this is what determines whether computers are useful or not. Secondly, the kind of support and service you have is probably more important than what brand it is. After all, if you can't make it work, who cares what brand it is? Most importantly, if you do a good job with planning and implementation, you should be able to succeed regardless of what computer you choose.

Reader: I see. Well, how about this question: What's the best way to use computers in a school?

Author: It depends on the school.

Reader: Like how?

Author: Like the teachers, students, facilities, budget. You would have to tell me what kind of computer experience the teachers had, what the major needs of the students were, what kind of school facilities you have, and what your budget for computing is. Most of all, I would need to know the problems and goals of the school. Then we could figure out the best use of computers for that school.

Reader: I'd love to, prof, but that sounds like it would take a little while. Let me just ask a few more questions, OK?

Author: No problem.

Reader: Here's a big one. How are we supposed to pay for all these computers, and is it really worth it?

Author: You're right, that is a pretty important question. The answer to the first part of the question is that we pay for the computers the same way we pay for all other aspects of the school system. The money comes from federal, state, and local funding sources. You budget for computer activities just like everything else.

Reader: Yeah, but how do I justify it. I mean, I can justify buildings, school buses, textbooks, salary increases, or athletic gear. But...computers?

Author: That's exactly my point.

Reader: What point?

Author: Once you understand the contribution that computers make to a school, they become as routine as everything else in the budget. The problem is that at this point, they don't seem very critical to you.

Reader: Well, that's probably true.

Author: Can I ask you a question?

Reader: Sure.

Author: Do you use computers yourself?

Reader: Yeah, I have one at home that I use for word processing and spreadsheets.

Author: Is it worthwhile? Can you imagine yourself using a typewriter or calculator instead of word processing and spreadsheets?

Reader: Not really. Yeah, its pretty valuable.

Author: So, why wouldn't it be just as valuable to all the students, teachers, and staff at school?

Reader: But that's different.

Author: Why?

Reader: Well, for one thing, where are they going to learn how to use computers like that? And how would they get enough time on a machine. And, what does that have to do with using computers for instructional purposes?

Author: Now those are really good questions. Do you think teachers could teach students how to use computers to solve problems and get things done in their subject areas? Do you think that you can figure out ways to provide every student with enough time on a computer to learn how to use it as a personal tool? Maybe there are a lot of different ways to use computers as part of the teaching/learning process?

Reader: Yeah, I suppose so. Look, prof, just answer one more question for me. What's in this for me?

Author: Oh, probably your career.

Reader: How's that?

Author: Like it or not, computers are here to stay. If you want to stay on top of things, be productive, and understand what's going on, you need to be comfortable with them. If you want to run a school properly, you need to use them and be sure that they are being used properly by teachers and students.

Reader: Boy, you put that pretty bluntly. How can you be so sure about all this?

Author: I saw it all in a dream. Besides, you want to risk it?

Reader: Not really. I guess I should read the rest of the book, eh?

Author: It might be a good idea. Just to hedge your bet.

Reader: At least, it's a short book.

1

Introduction

Computers have become pervasive in today's world. No matter what business or occupation you examine, you will find computers playing an important role. Statistics indicate that about half of the workforce use computers on a regular basis as part of their job: office workers, small business owners, factory workers, corporate executives, retail clerks, travel agents, bank tellers, physicians, police officers, sales representatives, service technicians, musicians, engineers, printers, soldiers, architects, journalists, farmers, politicians, stock brokers. As time goes on, most people will not only use a computer in their work, but also have one in their home.

Why have computers become so pervasive? There is a one word answer: productivity. Computers let people get things done in less time with better results. Indeed, in many cases, they allow people to accomplish tasks that they would not be able to do without the use of a computer. For example, think about what happens when a travel agent makes a plane reservation for you. Without the use of online databases, it is hard to imagine how our modern airline system could function. Or how about getting money from an automated bank machine? Not only is it fast, but you can do your banking anytime you want. Desktop publishing makes it possible for almost any personal computer owner to produce professionally printed documents in their office or home. All of these examples illustrate how computers have resulted in major changes to our lives and how we do things.

Which brings us to the subject of this book: How to improve the productivity of schools through computer technology. Computers have already become commonplace in schools; there are now almost two million machines in the nation's public school system (a ratio of about 1 computer per 30 students). While there are many examples of productivity gains in teaching and administration because of computers, the overall results have not been particularly impressive. Computers have not transformed the school system in the same way that they have dramatically altered most other aspects of society. What went wrong?

The lack of impact of computers in schools can be traced to a single fundamental problem: our failure to use them appropriately. Computers were perceived as instructional media to deliver drills and tutorials; as fancy calculators for math, statistics, or accounting; or as the means to teach everyone how to write BASIC programs. They were not seen as tools for writing, problem solving, decision making, data collection, creative expression, or communication. In other words, we got off on the wrong foot.

Underlying this misunderstanding was a profound lack of knowledge about computers on the part of teachers and school administrators. Schools bought machines and software and put them in classrooms and offices expecting that magic would happen. In a small number of cases it did. But in most schools, nothing of great value happened. Neither teachers nor administrators had any real idea of how to exploit the potential of the machines they had inherited. So the machines sat around unused or were abandoned.

Realizing the problem, school systems got busy on educating teachers about computers. Schools of education added computer courses to their teacher training. States mandated computer competencies for teacher credentials. Books and magazines about teaching with computers appeared by the dozens. During the 1980s more and more teachers became "computer literate" in some fashion.

Alas, little attention was paid to helping administrators become computer literate. There were very few inservice programs aimed at principals or superintendents. Schools of education did not add computing courses to administration programs. There were only a handful of books and magazines about educational computing for administrators.[1] Teachers were becoming pretty comfortable with

---

[1] See Bluhm (1987), Cheever (1986), Gustafson (1985), Miller (1988), or Radin and Greensberg (1982).

computers. Many students and parents already were. But the individuals responsible for leading and managing the school system were being left out in the dark.

This is where you and this book come in. If you are involved in educational administration at any level, you need to develop a sophisticated understanding of what computers can do and how they can be applied to education. If you are going to be responsible for administering schools full of computer literate teachers and students, then it follows that you better be computer literate yourself. Furthermore, everyone agrees that we need to increase the productivity of our school system. Computers can help do this in a big way, but only if their potential is properly understood. To make your school or school system more productive, you need the knowledge to make good decisions about computer use.

THE SCHOOL MILIEU

Before we start to talk about computers, let's discuss the milieu that school administrators find themselves in today. Here's a list of typical concerns:

- student/staff drug use
- teacher strikes/grievances
- educational excellence/accountability
- discontented parents/employers
- student vandalism/violence
- political/religious fanatics
- declining enrollments/budgets
- mainstreaming/special education
- racial/ethnic discrimination
- teacher apathy/burnout
- school board politics
- sexual/child abuse
- teenage pregnancy/child care
- AIDs.

Of course these issues are in addition to the routine tasks of operating a school or school system, such as budgets, staff supervision, scheduling, recruitment, and hosting visitors!

Into this milieu we add another element—computers. However, computers are not another issue or problem to be dealt with; they are part of the solution. All of the issues listed above require decisions and judgments based upon facts and information. The computer can play a role in collecting or analyzing such information. More importantly, the use of the computer to minimize the time spent on routine tasks can free up more time to deal with the difficult issues. In addition, there is a real possibility that meaningful use of computers in the classroom might alleviate some of the malaise that afflicts students and teachers.

It would be pure hogwash to suggest that computers are going to solve deep-rooted social and economic problems, such as drug abuse, racial discrimination, teacher grievances, or declining enrollments. Indeed, without deliberate intervention, computers may aggrevate existing problems further by increasing the gap between the haves and the have-nots. Classroom use of computers can reinforce gender bias, racial stereotypes, and the limitations placed on handicapped students. But it can also diminish the gap and minimize such differences. School administrators must ensure that computers are used as vehicles of opportunity, not instruments of oppression.

How can computers contribute to a school if used wisely? In the classroom, they can improve the quality of learning and teaching by making it more challenging, more relevant, and more rewarding (we will discuss how in Chapter 4). If successful, this may improve grades, reduce absenteeism, increase self-esteem, and cut discipline problems. Many of the payoffs of effective computer use are improved social skills and interaction, rather than better grades. For teachers, computers may increase their enthusiasm for teaching and improve their understanding of what they teach. This could translate into fewer burn-outs, less discontent, and reduced turnover.

In the front or district office, computers can significantly reduce the time required for repetitive chores, such as attendance reporting, form letters, payrolls, room scheduling, student registration, or grading. They can improve the accessibility of information on students or staff, budgets, expenses, supplies, equipment, and all forms of school records. They can also open up new opportunities for information access through online databases or for collaboration via electronic networks.

However, in order to realize the potential of computers in any school application, there are many new decisions to be made and additional planning steps. Hardware and software must be selected, special facilities are needed, teachers and staff must be trained, policies and procedures concerning computer use will be required, and so on. Computers are not a simple equipment addition; they typically involve major changes to the way a school is run and organized.

To summarize, computers do add more complexity to the job of an educational administrator. However, they provide a powerful tool that can be used to manage the overall complexity of the job, as well as improve the quality of classroom activities. Your task is to learn enough about computers to make them work for you, not against you.

WHAT YOU NEED TO KNOW

Educational administrators typically wear three hats: leader, manager, and politician. In the leadership role, the job of an administrator is to produce change in an organization—a particular school, a school district, or the overall school system. As a manager, the administrator must ensure that the organization runs smoothly and efficiently. Being a politician means achieving a balance between the interests of everyone involved in the school system and the surrounding community.

In the context of computers, each of these three roles relates to different responsibilities. The leadership role requires you to motivate others to embrace computer technology where appropriate and to remove any obstacles to computer use. As a manager, it behooves you to identify how computers can improve the efficiency of school operations and ensure that they are implemented successfully. Politically, you must adjudicate computer use so that it serves the interests and needs of all school constituents. In short, you should occupy a middle ground somewhere between being a technology zealot and a computer luddite!

To fulfill these responsibilities, here are a list of the specific competencies needed:

- be able to explain basic computer terms and concepts
- be able to describe major hardware and software components

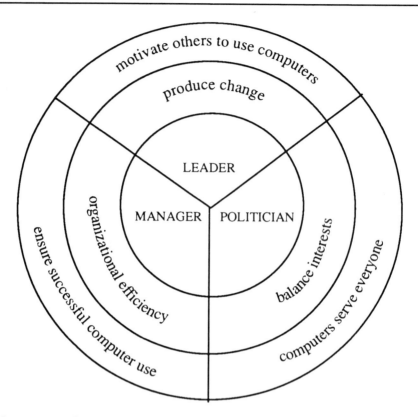

Figure 1.1. The major roles of educational administrators with respect to computers.

- understand the factors involved in evaluation/selection of hardware and software
- knowledge of administrative applications
- knowledge of instructional applications
- awareness of the social issues associated with computer use
- familarity with the factors that affect successful use of computers
- awareness of future developments in computers and education.

By the time you finish this book (especially if you work through some of the exercises provided at the end of each chapter), you should have acquired the knowledge necessary to use computers wisely in any educational setting. However, to really understand the power of computers, you need to use them personally. So just reading this book isn't enough. You need to spend enough time on a machine to become proficient with word processing, spreadsheets, database, and telecommunications software. Learning a good integrated program, such as Lotus 1-2-3 or Microsoft Works, will help you achieve this. Not only will you then understand computers at a "nuts and bolts" level, but you will also be able to improve your own productivity. And that is what computers are all about.

WHO SHOULD READ THIS BOOK?

This book will be worthwhile reading for anyone involved in the administration of schools, whether public or private, primary or secondary. This includes principals, department heads, superintendents, program directors, curriculum coordinators, and school board members. Teachers, teacher aides, librarians, and media specialists who have some administrative duties can also benefit from reading this book.

The book will also be of interest to college-level administrators and training managers. Although post-secondary institutions and corporate training centers differ from schools in many ways, the administrative applications of computers are essentially the same. The main difference is a matter of scale—activities, such as registration, class scheduling, budgeting, facilities management, and publishing, are likely to be more complex.

While not intended to be comprehensive, this book should be suitable as a text in an educational administration program. Since the book focuses in the global issues of administrative computing common to all grade levels and school systems, it will be useful for classes composed of administrators from different levels and different geographical areas or countries. Because the book does not cover instructional applications of computers in detail, it should not be used for training teachers about classroom use of computers; there are many suitable books for this purpose.[2] A set of exercises are provided at the end of each chapter to be used for class discussion, assignments, or self-evaluation.

Note that no computer background or experience is assumed in this book. If you know absolutely nothing about computers, this

---

[2] See Coburn et al. (1985), Collis (1988), Roberts, Carter, Friel, and Miller (1988), Turner and Land (1988), or Wright and Forcier (1985).

is the right book for you. On the other hand, if you already have some experience with computers, you should be able to get through the book a little faster, but still learn a lot about administrative applications.

ORGANIZATION OF THE BOOK

The rest of the book consists of the following chapters:

2. *How Can Computers Help?*—An overview of administrative programs for all aspects of school activities including: scheduling, budgeting, accounting, grading, record keeping, inventory, guidance, and libraries.
3. *Tools for Schools*—A discussion of how applications software (word processing, spreadsheets, databases) can be used for administrative activities.
4. *Computers in the Classroom*—Instructional applications and how to facilitate the classroom use of computers.
5. *Hardware and Software Alternatives*—Factors to consider in selecting hardware and software and what the choices are.
6. *Successful Computer Implementation*—A discussion of the major implementation issues: facilities, staffing, training, security, and maintenance.
7. *Planning for Computers*—The major aspects of planning for computers including: goals and objectives, acquiring hardware and software, scheduling implementation, evaluation and the development of policies and procedures.
8. *Financing Computers*—A discussion of cost/benefits analysis, budgeting, and funding sources.
9. *New Directions*—The likely impact of networks, laptops, hypertext, artificial intelligence, distance learning, and community outreach on computer use in schools.
10. *Welcome to P.S. 1991*—A case study of computer use in a hypothetical school that illustrates issues raised in earlier chapters.

Glossary: Brief explanations of important computer terms and concepts.

Appendix: Resources—Where to find out more about computers and educational administration.

By the way, you will notice that the book doesn't cover the history of computers, how computers work, or programming. While these topics may be of interest to some readers, they are not critical to knowing how to use computers for administrative applications. You do not have to become a computer technician in order to use computers, any more than you have to become an automotive mechanic in order to drive a car.

While the book does discuss different types of hardware and software, it does not discuss specific brands or program names. There are a variety of reasons for this. Such information is very transitory —machines and programs come and go with annoying rapidity. This information is better obtained from magazines, attending vendor exhibits at conferences, or via online databases (see the Appendix for some sources). If you understand the major concepts and categories of hardware and software, you will have no trouble identifying specific machines and programs when you need to.

We hope you will find this book useful in unleasing the power of computers to improve education and your own effectiveness as an administrator. Taming the computer can be an exciting challenge and a wonderful adventure. Of course, it is sometimes frustrating and bewildering. Just remember not to let the beast get you down; it's only a hunk of metal and plastic.

EXERCISES

1. Conduct an assessment of current and past computer activities in your school or school district. Talk to teachers, students, parents, school board members, and other administrators. What is the consensus about the value of these activities?

2. Pick some noneducational domain, such as agriculture, banking, transportation, manufacturing, or publishing, and identify the impact of computers in this domain. How have computers affected productivity? Are there any lessons for educational applications?

3. Over the decades ther have been many reform movements in education. Investigate the goals and methods of some of these movements. How do computer learning approaches compare?

4. Make a list of your daily administrative activities. Estimate the time spent on each activity. Which activities do you think

could be made more productive using computers? How much time could be saved? Which activities would get done better?

5. Develop three scenarios about computer use in your school or school district: a worst case, a best case, and a likely case. Identify the factors that determine each outcome.

6. Make a list of as many occupations as you can. Beside each occupation, identify the nature of computer use involved, if any. How well does the present school or college curriculum prepare students for the computer skills needed for each job you have listed?

2

How Can Computers Help?

Educational administrators are responsible for managing their school or school system. This involves supervising routine functions, solving problems, and making decisions. To perform these duties administrators need information—data and facts upon which decisions and actions can be based. One of the most important ways that computers can improve school productivity is to make information more available, faster to obtain, or easier to understand. In practice, this means the creation and use of databases and printed reports.

Over the past two decades, a large number of computer programs have been developed and used for a variety of school functions. This includes: accounting, scheduling, attendance, grading, inventory, student information systems, library use, guidance, transportation management, food services, energy monitoring, and decision support systems. In this chapter, we provide an overview of the capabilities and limitations of programs for these applications.

ACCOUNTING

Schools are businesses, and educational administrators must ensure that all financial aspects are run smoothly. In large schools and school districts, there will be a business manager who is dedicated to the management of financial operations; in smaller schools and districts, principals and superintendents will have responsibility for "juggling the books." Regardless of the size of the school or district, computers have become indispensible for carrying out the full range of accounting functions.

Payroll

Since the majority of a school budget goes to payroll, it should be no surprise that this function is a high priority for automation. A payroll system tracks the amount of time worked by each school employee, generates paychecks, produces tax reports and W-2s, and generates wage statistics according to accounts or employee characteristics. Instead of printing checks, pay may be electronically transferred to an employee's bank account.

Because of the many deductions involved, payroll calculations are complicated. Furthermore, they must be completely accurate and free of any errors. These criteria make payroll a perfect candidate for computerization.

Purchasing

Purchasing supplies and services requires a system to track the status of orders and to generate purchase orders. For larger items, it will be necessary to generate bid requests. When an item is requested by a teacher or staff member, a requisition form is normally completed. After approval, the requisition is entered into the system and a purchase order or bid request is printed.

A purchasing system can provide many additional capabilities that streamline the ordering process. For example, the system can keep a database of specifications for regularly ordered items that saves the trouble of entering descriptions each time. The system can automatically identify overdue orders. If connected up to the inventory system, it can identify when supplies of stock items are low and should be reordered. When connected up to the general ledger, it can generate reports comparing actual and budgeted expenditures. In some systems, requisitions are entered online, reducing the time required to process orders and the paperwork involved.

Accounts Payable / Receivable

Accounts payable refers to a system that keeps track of all monies owed by a school and produces checks to pay invoices. Accounts receivable tracks money owed to the school and the generation of receipts. Public schools normally do not have many revenue transactions, so accounts receivable is usually a minor consideration. Accounts payable, however, can be quite complicated with hundreds of bills to pay every month. In private schools and higher education, accounts receivable and billing are a major undertaking since tuition for every student must be collected.

The main value of computerized accounts payable/receivable systems is that all entries can automatically be posted to the general ledger, saving a lot of tedious hand entries. The automatic generation of checks and status reports also saves time and ensures accuracy.

General Ledger

The general ledger is a statement of how debits and credits, assets and liabilities, or income and expenses, balance. It represents a key report for evaluating financial health relative to budgets and appropriations. Input to the general ledger comes from accounts payable/receivable, payroll, purchasing, and inventory. To the extent that all of these other accounting functions are automated, posting entries to the general ledger is simple.

The most important function of a general ledger program is the generation of reports, including expenditures by programs, balance sheets, audit reports, general journal summaries, and year-to-date reports. Many of these reports will be required by state or federal agencies and it is important that the system can generate them in the appropriate format.

Inventory

Inventory programs keep track of all school equipment and supplies. They usually indicate quantity, location, supplier, ordering/serial numbers, cost, date of purchase, and date of last inventory entry. Using an automated inventory system should make it easier to locate equipment, maintain supplies, complete insurance reports, and track losses. Inventory systems work best when they are linked up to purchasing and general ledger programs. New equipment and supplies can automatically be added to inventory when acquired as well as showing up as expenditures or assets.

At the district level, a separate inventory of capital (or fixed) assets may be kept. Capital assets include buildings, furnishings, machinery, vehicles, and land. These assets are subject to maintenance and depreciation, factors which involve additional accounting considerations. Inventory programs that are designed to handle capital assets would include procedures and reports for these special considerations.

Summary

While accounting functions represent a relatively mundane aspect of computer applications, they are a vital part of successful school operations and an area where computers can make significant contributions to productivity. As long as computer-based systems are implemented properly (discussed in Chapter 6), they allow accounting tasks to be carried out in a fraction of the time required for manual procedures with a high degree of accuracy and reliability.

In large public school systems, most accounting functions tend to be done at a district level by a data processing department or service. Individual schools typically access the system via terminals linked to a mainframe located in a district office. However, all of the functions discussed in this section can be accomplished using programs that run on personal computers. This allows schools to do any or all accounting functions themselves if they desire. Private schools and small colleges can take advantage of computer-based accounting for a minimum cost.

ATTENDANCE

Another important administrative task that computers can be applied to is attendance tracking and reporting. Schools are required by state laws to keep attendance records, which are used as the basis for determining financial support. Of course, attendance reports are also needed to assess student deportment in terms of lates and absences. Such information is likely to be used by principals, guidance counselors, and teachers. Attendance reporting systems provide school administrators with a powerful tool to help deal with a major school problem: absenteeism.

In addition to the need for complete accuracy, attendance data must be cumulated for various kinds of monthly, quarterly, and annual reports. These requirements make it an ideal application for computerization. Attendance data are often recorded on cards that can be optically scanned, minimizing the time required for data entry. Various kinds of reports can be generated based upon the number and type of absences or lates identified. Some programs can automatically create letters to parents that report their child's attendance records. When linked up to an automatic phone dialing system, some programs can actually call parents when a student is absent and deliver a recorded message notifying them of the absence.

Attendance programs illustrate one of the major benefits of many computer applications—the generation of reports. Once the data have been entered into the database, it becomes possible to print a variety of reports that show attendance statistics in different ways. In many cases, new reporting or analysis capabilities are made available that were not feasible by manual methods. However, these new reporting capabilities do not automatically translate into better administration; they merely provide information upon which to base actions. For example, an attendance program that generates parent notification letters provides an opportunity for follow-up activities on the part of the parent—the follow-up activities must be effective if they are to impact student attendance.

GRADING

Grade reporting is another important student data activity. Reasons for using a computer-based grading system are essentially the same as for attendance: accuracy and the wide variety of reports that can be generated. In addition to the student's report cards, the program can produce grade distribution summaries, honor rolls, eligibility lists, and demographic analyses.

In order to use a computer grading program, it is necessary to specify the format to be used by teachers to report the grade data, the grading scales, and the format for the report cards and other reports to be generated. Like registration and attendance data, grades can be provided on optical scoring sheets to speed up the data entry process. However, report cards must also convey teacher's comments, and scoring sheets must provide space for this. Some programs provide codes for a selection of standard comments with the option to add original remarks if desired.

One of the most valuable benefits of a computerized grading system is the quick turnaround time that is possible between the time the grades are submitted and the reports are printed. In some cases (such as high school graduation), there is an urgency for the final grade reports—the computer can process the grades and print reports in a matter of hours.

SCHEDULING

At the high school and college level, one of the most critical administrative tasks is student and class scheduling. Schedules define the educational activities of students and teachers as well as dictate the use of school facilities and equipment. The scheduling process must take into account the following considerations:

- student choice in the selection of courses
- curriculum prerequisites/requirements
- teacher qualifications and preferences
- optimal utilization of classrooms and facilities
- state/federal standards for time allocations
- appropriate lunch and study periods
- good balance in class sections
- provisions for special events (assemblies/athletics).

Scheduling systems must also be able to accommodate changes as students revise their programs, courses are added/dropped, rooms and facilities become unavailable, and teachers/staff come and go.

When a computer is used for scheduling, the following steps are usually involved:

KEEPING TRACK OF PEOPLE*

The Orange County school district in Orlando Florida employs over 12,000 people, about half of whom are teachers. Approximately 1,500 new employees are hired each year and about 1,300 leave. A personnel staff of 30 (a ratio of 1 to 400 employees) is able to handle all aspects of employment. Their secret is a sophisticated human resource management system. Before the system was implemented, processing a new teacher's papers used to take three weeks; now it takes a day.

When a teacher files an employment application, personnel staff type the application information into the system which runs on the district's mainframe. Principals and department heads at schools can then sign on to their terminals and view the application. If a principal decides to recommend hiring a particular applicant, he/she simply selects that option on the screen and the system records the principal's choice. A report is then run at the district that shows the status of each applicant. Hiring recommendations are then forwarded to the school board for approval. After the applicant is approved, the personnel file is transferred to payroll electronically so no rekeying of information is required.

The system is also used for other employment transactions, including salary increases, transfers, or termination. The employee's supervisor signs on to a terminal, selects the appropriate option, and completes any information needed. The recommended action is printed out in a report, reviewed by the personnel staff, and sent to the school board for approval. Because everything is done online, the time-consuming step of retyping forms is eliminated.

In addition to employment transactions, the system keeps track of payroll history and generates payroll checks. it is

* Source: From "Automating the Human Perspective," by K. Knauth, Electronic Learning, September 1989 (Special Supplement).

(continued)

19

also used to keep teachers informed of their certification status. When a teacher's certification is about to expire, the system produces a letter reminding them to recertify. Since all of the information is kept in a single database, it is possible to use the same system for many different purposes.

While the time savings in processing employee information is one of the obvious benefits of this kind of computer system, there is another, less obvious, but very important payoff. Because they spend less time completing forms, the personnel staff are able to spend more time talking to employees. The increase in personal attention goes hand-in-hand with personnel automation.

STUDENT INFORMATION SYSTEMS

When a school or school district starts to use a number of the applications discussed in this chapter, it soon becomes highly desirable to integrate all of the information about students into a single database, rather than have separate files for attendance, grades, test scores, and so on. Such an integrated database is called a student information system. The record for each student would typically include: demographic information (such as address, parent's place of work, birthdate), health records, attendance, schedule, grades, test scores, extracurricular activities, past courses, library usage, and guidance records. In the case of special education, Individual Educational Plans (IEPs) would also be included in the student's record. Figure 2.1 shows sample screen displays from a student information system that runs on personal computers.

From such a database, a wide variety of reports on the student body can be generated: student directories, bus assignments, parent letters, immunization lists, guidance appointments, grading comparisons, and graduation lists. In addition, all of the attendance, grading, and test score reports already discussed would be available. Most student information systems provide online access to the database that allows immediate display of the information desired.

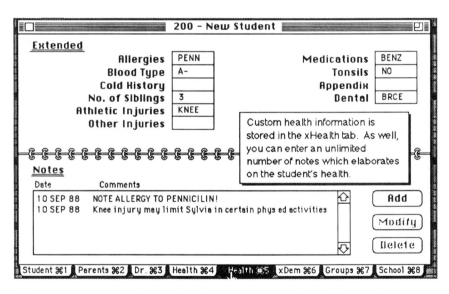

Figure 2.1. Screens from School System II, a student information system (Credit: Columbia Computing Systems).

The use of a student information system raises many policy and procedure issues. First and foremost is the issue of who may access the system and what privileges do they have. Obviously, the right to enter and modify attendance, grade, and test data should be limited since accidental or malicious changes could be very serious. On the other hand, to be most useful, all staff members will probably need access. The solution to this dilemma is to provide read-only access to most people and the capability to enter or change records to relatively few individuals in senior positions. Administrators must develop procedures and policies that ensure the privacy and security of student databases.

Another major issue that surfaces with student information systems is the question of where they should reside. Because of the amount of data and processing involved, they have historically required a relatively large system and were always a district level capability. Now such systems can run on a personal computer and be located at individual schools. Wrangles over what information and capabilities should be at the school versus district level are a routine aspect of the administrative computing scene. In general, schools want all the capability they can get since this gives them control of and immediate access to data.

Efficient use of a student database usually involves access from multiple terminals, and hence, a networked system. If the system resides at the district level, individual schools can access the system via telecommunication links. If the system is at the school level, a local network is typically involved. In either case, networking makes computer use and support more complicated.[3]

OTHER APPLICATIONS

Library Circulation and Cataloging

Many programs are available that allow librarians to track circulation of materials and to print overdue notices. If online cataloging is included, it becomes possible to search for materials by author, title, keyword, publisher, and subject. In addition, reports can be printed that list materials available by age or grade level. Such reports are useful to teachers who want to generate reading lists for students. Materials can also be tagged with bar-coded identification

[3] See Bank and Williams (1987), and Forman (1983), or Smith and Kauffman (1985) for further discussion of networking.

labels that expedite check-out. The net effect of these computer-based systems is to increase the efficiency of a library, while minimizing the staff required (and hence, costs). Online database services can vastly extend the information available to students and staff, but may be too expensive for most schools.

Guidance / Counseling

Various programs are available to help with guidance and counseling activities. Some programs attempt to help the student define vocational or academic interests by matching their profiles with occupational/educational descriptions. Other programs provide occupational/academic databases that list actual job opportunities or specific college programs and requirements. Such programs are not intended to be substitutes for human counselors, but to be tools that allow a counselor to provide students with a broader range of options. For schools that cannot afford to provide full-time counselors or must cut back on guidance services, computer-based counseling systems may help fill the gap.

Food Services

Food services constitute an important aspect of school operations that must adhere to various federal, state, and local policies. Administration of food services covers staffing, inventory, purchasing, menu management, accounting, and food preparation. While many of these functions overlap with general school functions (e.g., staffing, inventory, accounting), a good case can be made to treat food services separately. To facilitate this, there are numerous programs available that handle some or all food services activities. The Food and Nutrition Service of the U.S. Department of Agriculture has been an active participant in the development and dissemination of these programs.

Transportation

School buses are an essential element of most school systems, in terms of getting students to school and meeting desegregation requirements. Critical to a smoothly functioning bus system are efficient routine schedules and accurate tracking or maintenance operations. Many programs are available for these two functions. Routing programs generate schedules that minimize the mileage and waiting times for students, as well as printing reports that show pick-up times, mileage by bus, and route listings for drivers. Maintenance programs provide records on fuel usage, repairs and check-ups made, parts replaced, and the number of hours involved in maintenance. Some programs generate maintenance schedules indicating which buses need what service, and they can identify what parts and supplies should be ordered. With such a system in place, a transportation manager should be able to answer questions such as: (1) what maintenance activities take the most time or are most costly; (2) which buses should be replaced and when; and (3) are all types of buses performing equally well?

Energy Management

Energy crises and diminishing budgets have focused attention on energy conservation practices. Energy monitoring programs can be used to: (1) schedule the starting/stopping times for heating and cooling equipment to maintain an acceptable temperature range; (2) determine how many units should be operating at one time; or (3) limit electrical demand to cut excess usage charges. Reports on energy usage can pinpoint problems in building design, room utilization, and heating/cooling equipment.

Design Support Systems

One of the major problems facing most administrators in large school districts and at the college/university level is "information overload." As more and more computer systems of the kind mentioned in this chapter are put into place, administrators are confronted with enormous amounts of detailed data to analyze and make sense of. One solution to this dilemma is to use the computer itself to help analyze and organize the raw data. This is called a Decision Support System (DSS) and is a common data processing function in most large organizations. A DSS integrates information from multiple sources and produces concise reports to be used in decision making and planning. This allows an administrator to look at aggregate data across time as well as detailed daily information.[4]

SUMMARY

This chapter briefly introduced you to the diversity of administrative computing programs available.[5] In general, the benefits are the same for each application area: less time to process data, easier accessibility of information, and automatic printing of reports. These benefits add up to increased productivity in school operations. In many cases, the computerization of a task makes it possible to do things that would or could not be done otherwise. Examples include: the automatic generation of letters to parents concerning student absences, availability of test scores or grades the day after the raw data are turned in, automatic generation of bid requests from purchase orders, or reports on energy utilization in a school.

However, it is unlikely that the benefits possible from computerization will be realized without careful planning. Before purchasing any program, it is necessary to know exactly what kind of data are currently available, and what kind of reports are desired. Otherwise, you may purchase a program that does not work with the information currently available, or does not produce the kinds of reports wanted. Furthermore, it is important to determine the kinds of skills and training required to use a certain program before it is purchased. Different staffing may be needed for the computerized version of a task than when it was done manually.[6] These and other implementation considerations are discussed further in Chapter 6.

Buying programs that are specialized for a given school task has a number of advantages and disadvantages. The main advantage is that the program is ready to use and comes with documentation and training materials. This means that you can start the implementation process immediately. Other advantages include: the purchase or licensing price is clearly defined and can be budgeted

---

[4] See Turban (1988) for an overview of Decision Support Systems.
[5] For further discussion of administrative software, see Pogrow (1984, 1985).
[6] See Church and Bender (1985) for further discussion of this.

for; the vendor should provide support; and it is possible to see the system in use at other sites before implementing it yourself. The main disadvantage of buying specialized programs is that they may not be flexible enough to accommodate all of your current or future requirements. Additional problems may include: incompatibility with other programs in use, difficulty in getting support from the vendor, and the cost of the software.

In the next chapter, we discuss general purpose application programs. In almost all cases, these programs can be used for the kinds of applications discussed in this chapter. However, someone has to learn the applications programs well enough to use them. In most cases, specialized programs are much faster to learn and easier to use for the function they are designed for. However, general purpose programs provide more flexibility and better data-sharing capabilities. One of the jobs of a computer literate administrator is to be able to make tradeoff decisions between the use of specialized and general purpose programs for a particular school application.

EXERCISES

1. Most of the applications discussed in this chapter could be implemented at the school or district level. Make a list showing which level would be most appropriate for each application in your own school system.
2. Prioritize the applications discussed in this chapter in terms of need for your own school or school district. To do this, rate each application in terms of the problem(s) it addresses, the expected benefits, and whom it would benefit.
3. Choose one application discussed in this chapter and make a detailed list of the steps involved in doing the task in its current form. Estimate the amount of time required for each step. Make a list of the steps involved if the task was automated, and estimate times using a specific system. Does computerization save time?
4. Choose one application discussed in this chapter and write a scenario of how it could be used in your school or school district. Circulate this description to some teachers, staff, students,

parents, and fellow administrators for their comments. Ask if they would support this computer use and why/why not. Summarize their comments.

5. When tasks are automated, some things get left out or overlooked. Make a list of such considerations for one or more applications discussed in this chapter based upon your experience or that of others. How serious is the omission of these factors?

CHECKLIST FOR ADMINISTRATIVE SOFTWARE

Accounting

- ☐ Better accuracy needed?
- ☐ Not able to keep up with the workload?
- ☐ Need better access to financial information?

Attendance

- ☐ Too much time typing reports?
- ☐ Better accuracy needed?
- ☐ Better parent notification desirable?

Grading

- ☐ Faster turnaround desired?
- ☐ Better accuracy desired?

Scheduling

- ☐ More flexible timetables desired?
- ☐ Faster turnaround desired?

Test Scoring

- ☐ Better analysis of data desirable?
- ☐ Ability to process tests faster?

(continued)

Student Information System

- ☐ Better access to data required?
- ☐ Difficulty finding information when needed?

Other Applications Desirable?

- ☐ Library
- ☐ Guidance
- ☐ Food Services
- ☐ Transportation
- ☐ Energy Management
- ☐ Decision Support System

3

Tools for Schools

In the preceding chapter, we discussed the range of possible applications of computers in school administration. In this chapter, we look at general purpose programs and how they can be used for some of the applications as well as other tasks. Since many of these programs can also be used for instructional activities, this chapter provides a transition for Chapter 4.

WORD PROCESSING AND DESKTOP PUBLISHING

To the extent that administration involves a great deal of paperwork, word processing is one of the most important ways that computers can improve administrative productivity. Using a word processor reduces the amount of time required to make revisions to a document and improves the quality at the same time. These benefits derive from the ease of making changes to a previously typed document and the professional looking output produced by computer printers.

Word processing programs consist of two major capabilities: editing and formatting. The editing component allows you to insert, delete, copy, or move any aspect of a document from characters to paragraphs with a few key strokes. Formatting allows you to automatically set margins, page lengths, justification, line spacing, and headers/footers. When you print a document, it comes out according to the format you have specified, regardless of how you typed it in originally. In addition to the editing and formatting capabilities,

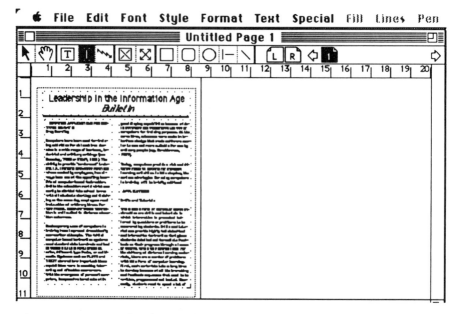

Figure 3.1.   Example of a page layout program used for desktop publishing, Ready Set Go (Credit: LetraSet Corp.)

word processing programs have a search-and-replace feature that lets you find any text string in a document and replace it throughout the document. Most word processing programs now include a spelling checker that highlights misspelled words; this results in better quality documents.

More recent word processing programs allow you to control the typography of the document (i.e., type style and size), as well as the number of columns and the insertion of graphics. Desktop publishing software takes word processing one step further by letting you arrange the layout of a page in terms of blocks of texts and graphics (see Figure 3.1). If you are creating a newsletter, brochure, form, or yearbook, the added capabilities of a desktop publishing program are highly desirable.

There are many ways that word processing saves time. Once you have created a document, you can reuse that same document many times by making small changes. For example, teacher or parent memos that you send frequently only need a new date, address, and possibly addition of a new sentence or two, and then they are ready to print. Furthermore, it is easy to compose new documents from pieces of existing ones. So, you might create a new proposal by combining sections from other proposals you have already done. This electronic "cut and paste" capability can save a great deal of time that would be wasted starting from scratch.

One standard word processing technique is to compose a "master" document that contains all typical components for that purpose and then you select from these components every time you need that type of document. For example, you might compose a teacher evaluation master that contains all of the usual problems and recommendations. To create an evaluation letter for a teacher, you simply select the phrases that are relevant, add anything unique for this teacher, and print it out. This method saves retyping the same things over and over and speeds up the evaluation process.[1]

Another important capability of word processing is "mail merge" which allows you to send the same letter to many people with the address and other information in the body of the letter (such as student grade or attendance reports) to be taken from a database or mailing list file. Once this capability has been set up, hundreds or thousands of letters can be printed in a matter of hours.

Of course, there are drawbacks and limitations to word processing. First, learning a new word processor requires a substantial investment of time. Luckily, once you have learned one word processing program, learning another is fairly easy since the same basic concepts are involved. Another problem is losing documents. Everyone who uses a word processor sooner or later has the horrible experience of forgetting to save their file (or accidently erasing it) and losing many hours of work. Such experiences teach you to be more careful about saving and "backing up" files. When there are problems with equipment, such as disk drives or printers, it may be difficult or impossible to get work accomplished. Again, the wise computer user learns lessons (in this case, about having redundant equipment) that can minimize the significance of such problems.

One of the major implementation issues to be decided upon with word processing is who uses it. In the classic office model, all typing is done by clerks and secretaries. However, with word processing, there are many instances where it is easier and faster for the creator to type the document personally rather than write it out first. This is especially true when a document is mostly composed from already

---

[1] See Pennington (1984) for further discussion of this idea.

existing masters. So, it makes sense for most administrators to learn how to use word processing programs and have a computer of their own. However, it is important that they use the same type of word processing program as the rest of the staff, otherwise there may be file compatibility problems (see Chapter 5).

Everything we have just discussed about word processing applies equally well to desktop publishing, with a few extra wrinkles. Learning to use a desktop publishing program requires a long time and also requires a knowledge of page layout principles. Graphics design skills are very important in creating good looking documents. So, while just about anybody can use a desktop publishing program, the right background and training are essential to really use it properly.

DATABASE MANAGEMENT

Next to creating documents, the most common task in school administration is keeping records and looking up information. In computer terms, record-keeping systems are called database management programs. You have already been introduced to some special purpose database management programs in Chapter 2—attendance, grading, inventory, and student information systems.

A database management program lets you specify what kind of information you want to keep and how you want it printed out in the form of reports. Most database programs also let you specify what the information looks like on the screen when it is entered or displayed. When you create a database, you define the fields associated with each record (e.g., names addresses, phone numbers, etc.), the length of the fields, and their layout on the screen. You also define what fields are to be printed in reports and their layout. Once the database is defined, you can start entering information.

Apart from printing reports, there are two major capabilities of a database management program that are important—searching and sorting. Searching refers to the functions that allow you to look up information in the database. Sorting functions let you rearrange or select information according to certain "keys" that you provide. In both searching and sorting capability, you want as much flexibility as possible. For example, you might want to find all teachers who received their certification before or after a certain date. Or, you might want a list of all parents sorted by zip code or street addresses. To perform these kind of searches and sorts, you need the capability to specify AND/OR combinations and make numerical comparisons.

Relational database programs allow you to compare information across two or more different files. For example, suppose that you wanted to correlate information from attendance files with information from grading or demographic files. By using a field common to all files (in this case, student name or ID), you could select the information desired. Relational databases make it easier to keep information up to date since changes to all related fields are made simultaneously. Many relational databases provide an English-like query language that makes it easy to phrase search requests.

The power of a database management program is that once the data are entered into the program, you can find information and produce reports in a matter of seconds. Suppose that you suddenly had a TB scare in your school and needed a list of which students had been previously innoculated. If student health records are in the database, you simply have to request a printout and you have the information needed. Or, imagine that a school district is going to be subdivided and you need to know how many students would be affected by the change. You could sort students by street names and produce a list of those affected.

The examples above also illustrate the biggest limitation of using a database management program: you can't work with data that are not in the database. When setting up a database, you need to carefully think through the possible uses of the program to be sure that all data needed will be included. In the case of functions that have been done manually, this is not hard since the kinds or reports and information requests involved will be well-known. However, when setting up a database for something new, it will be much harder to predict what information will be needed. While the information can always be added later, it is often inconvenient and more time-consuming.

An issue of special importance with database programs is security. Since much of the data kept in databases are of a confidential nature, it is essential to take certain precautions in terms of who has access to database programs. Passwords are typically used to prevent unauthorized access. Many programs allow different levels of access to be defined—differentiating those users who can enter and change data from those who can only perform searches and print reports. In addition, backup of files must be routine so that there is always another copy of each database.

SPREADSHEETS

A third program of importance to educational administrators is the electronic spreadsheet program. Spreadsheets are general purpose decision tools that can be used for a variety of purposes: budgets, schedules, workplans, forecasting, evaluations, and accounting functions. Their power and versatility are made possible by their simple design: rows and columns that can be defined in any fashion, and a set of functions that allow each cell defined by a row and a column to be computed in different ways. Formulas can be defined and applied to individual cells or entire rows and columns. Entries in any cell can be numbers, text, or formula.

One of the most powerful features of a spreadsheet is that data can be recalculated instantly. For example, suppose that you have entered data for an annual budget with each row representing a line item and the columns representing months. The last row and column would be defined as the total. If you change the entry in a specific cell, all of the totals will immediately be recalculated to show the new totals. Or, if you delete or add a row, the totals would be automatically recalculated to reflect the deletion or addition. This automatic recalculation capability makes spreadsheets ideal for "what if" exploration—changing numbers and assumptions to see how it affects the bottom line or other components.

Typical kinds of "what-if" capabilities that a school administrator might want to investigate are:

- What are the effects of losing/gaining a certain number of students?
- If faculty or staff are given a certain pay raise, how would that affect the budget?
- How would the budget be affected by a increase or decrease in state/federal aid?
- How will class/teacher loads be affected by adding/losing a certain number of aids?

- How would new equipment or facilities affect the budget or the tax rate?
- If work schedules are changed, how would this affect payroll?

While spreadsheets do not usually provide the direct answer to a question, they provide the data analysis capability needed to reach a conclusion.[2]

Spreadsheet programs provide options that allow you to change the width of columns, define the type of data in cells (e.g., integers, decimals, dollars), justify the cell entries, and "protect" cells from being changed. Built-in functions are provided for calculating averages, totals, square roots, and other mathematical operations. There are also functions to duplicate or move entries and to print out all parts of a spreadsheet. Many spreadsheets allow you to specify logic in your functions so that you write "If . . . then" branches as part of the calculations. Most recent programs include graphing capabilities so you can produce graphs and charts directly from the data in the spreadsheet, as well as the capability to define the type style and size of information in the spreadsheet.

Once a "template" is created for a particular activity, it can be saved and reused as often as needed. This is analogous to using a master copy of a document in word processing. Using a template, the old data can be erased and new data entered without affecting the formulas and headings. Data from more than one spreadsheet can be combined to allow calculations across different sets of data. Ready-made templates can be bought from commercial sources for many applications.

While learning to use a spreadsheet program does not take a long time, learning how to use one well can take a while. Setting up a complex spreadsheet with many calculations and formula can be very time-consuming. One of the major concerns in creating a new spreadsheet is to ensure that all formulas are correct. This requires a lot of testing with known results.

Spreadsheets make financial analyses much easier than manual methods. Furthermore, they give administrators a real sense of power over the budgets they are responsible for. By knowing how the numbers are arrived at, and what affects what, administrators

---

[2] See Kacanek (1984) for a discussion of how to use spreadsheets for projecting enrollments.

are able to understand their financial statements and make better decisions. For this reason, the use of spreadsheets is a very important asset for administrators.

GRAPHICS AND DESKTOP PRESENTATIONS

Most educational administrators spend a lot of time making presentations to school boards, parents, community groups, state agencies, or teachers. These presentations require high quality visuals in order to communicate ideas in an effective manner. Various programs are available that facilitate the development and delivery of such presentations.

Graphing programs automatically produce graphs, bar charts, and pie charts from data entered into the program. These types of graphs and charts are useful for depicting budget breakdowns, trends in student data, such as enrollments or attendance, building or vehicle utilization, and demographic statistics. Input data for graphing programs may come from spreadsheet or database files.

Graphics editors are programs that allow you to create screens with any kind of text or illustrations desired. These programs provide a "toolbox" of different functions that produce lines, boxes, circles, patterns, shading, or different type fonts (see Figure 3.2). Freehand drawing is made possible using a mouse or the cursor keys. Collections of electronic "clip-art" provide ready-made illustrations that can be used in composing graphics.

Desktop presentation software (also called "storyboard" programs) allow you to arrange graphic screens created with a graphics editor or graphing program into an electronic slide presentation that can be displayed using a large screen projector or LCD tablet (see Chapter 5). Desktop presentation programs allow you to sequence the screens and control the display timing. They also provide special effects (e.g., "wipes" and "splits") and printing capabilities.

The major benefit of using graphics and desktop presentation software is these programs allow you to create professional looking materials quickly and inexpensively. Without the use of such programs, the visuals used in presentations tend to be poor in quality, difficult to read, fail to capture attention, and don't convey the

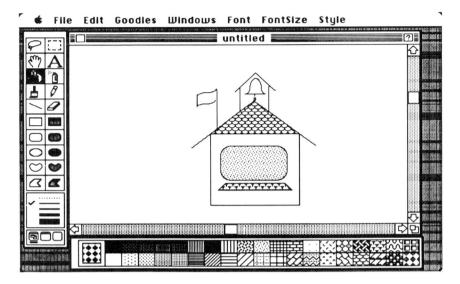

Figure 3.2. Example of a graphics editor program, Full Paint (Credit: Ann Arbor Software).

ideas intended. On the other hand, it takes time to produce interesting graphics, and requires graphics design skill. Use of graphics and desktop presentation software does not magically produce good visuals, but it does make it faster and easier.

TELECOMMUNICATIONS

One of the major breakthroughs that computers have introduced is electronic communications—the capability to transfer information between computers. Electronic message systems allow people to send and receive electronic mail and participate in computer conferences independent of their geographical location or time zones. Using electronic mail, it becomes possible for a group of individuals to carry on an intensive discussion or share ideas even though they may be in different places at different times. Unlike telephone interactions, people do not have to be available at the same time, but can participate as their schedules permit. Given the hectic pace of a typical administrator's day, this is an important capability.

Another important aspect of electronic communications is access to and use of online databases. There are literally thousands of online databases available providing information ranging from journal abstracts to economic statistics. Some of the better known database systems include DIALOG, BRS, and NEXIS. Most of these systems provide access to the ERIC database as well as other abstracting services of interest to education.[3] Online databases are a natural addition to a school library, and many library specialists are knowledgeable about how to use these systems.

Access to electronic message and online database systems is made possible by telecommunications software and a modem (modems are discussed in Chapter 5). Telecommunications programs allow you to sign on to networks, transfer files, and save information to disk. They also let you store the phone numbers of networks and take care of some or all of the sign-on process.

The use of electronic communications opens up new channels of communication and sources of information for educators. While telecommunications software is not difficult to use, it does take some practice and an understanding of how electronic communications work. The major obstacle to the use of computer telecommunications is cost. Usage charges tend to be in the $5–$20 per hour range, and regular use by students or teachers can be expensive. On the other hand, there are many cases where the benefits of electronic messaging or online databases are unique and worth their cost. Cost/benefits are discussed further in Chapter 8.

INTEGRATED SOFTWARE

To this point, we have discussed each of the major types of software in isolation. However, there are many cases when you want to transfer data from one program to another. The example of graphing results produced in a spreadsheet has already been mentioned earlier. Another common situation is the inclusion of spreadsheet, database, or graphics information in a report created with a word processing program. Or consider the case of wanting to move database information into a spreadsheet or vice-versa. And, once you

---

[3] For a good introduction to the commercial networks and telecommunications, see Glossbrenner (1983).

start using electronic communications, you may want to transfer the results from any program to somewhere else using telecommunications software.

In short, there is a need to be able to move data back and forth between programs. This is accomplished most easily by so-called integrated software that includes word processing, database management, spreadsheet, graphics, and telecommunications programs all in one program.[4] These programs make it easy to go back and forth between different applications. More importantly, they minimize learning time since each application works the same way as the others. It is not necessary to learn a different program for each application. Integrated programs represent a cost-effective and convenient solution to using applications software.

SUMMARY

This chapter discussed the nature and benefits of using applications software for educational administration. In general, the benefits include the ability to get work done in less time, to be able to do things not previously possible, and to produce better results than before. There are many examples of administrators who have produced documents, reports, or financial analyses that they could not or would not have been able to do without the use of computers.

There are also common problems in using applications software. Programs take time to learn and require practice before they can be used effectively. Additional time is required to set up databases or spreadsheets. Sometimes programs cannot do what is desired. And, if reasonable precautions aren't taken to save work and backup files regularly, work can be lost.

An ongoing dilemma facing administrators who use computers is whether to use general purpose software or special purpose programs for a given task. It should be clear to you that the applications programs discussed in this chapter could be used for many of the functions discussed in the previous chapter. General purpose programs usually provide more flexibility since you get to do it the

---

[4] Some popular examples of integrated programs are Lotus 1-2-3 for IBM PCs, Microsoft Works for the Apple Macintosh, and AppleWorks for the Apple II computers.

way you want. On the other hand, a considerable amount of time (and expertise) may be required to set up the program to do what you want. Specialized programs can be used immediately and are usually well-documented and supported. You will have to make this tradeoff decision for each administrative task you consider using computers for.

EXERCISES

1.   Make a list of things that you think you could accomplish more effectively using each of the applications programs discussed in this chapter. What tasks do you feel would not be done better using a computer?

2.   Take one task that you presently do by hand, and automate it using one of the types of applications programs discussed in this chapter. After you are done, analyze the advantages and disadvantages of computerization for this example.

3.   Find someone who uses applications progams on a regular basis. Interview them to identify what they feel are the major benefits and limitations of using such programs. Ask them what additional features or capabilities would make their computer use more effective.

4.   Select a particular administrative task and compare the use of a general purpose versus specialized program for that task. You will need to research the capabilities of the specialized programs, as well as identify the steps taken in using a general purpose program.

5.   Conduct a study to determine the most suitable integrated program for use in your school or district. Compare it to the use of separate programs for each application area. What would you recommend using?

6.   Make a list of the advantages and disadvantages of using the same applications software as your teachers and students use in the classroom. Think about how your needs and those of the classroom compare.

CHECKLIST FOR APPLICATIONS SOFTWARE

Word Processing/Desktop Publishing

☐ Basic editing and formatting capabilities?
☐ Control of typography (text fonts and styles)?
☐ Control of page layout (columns, graphics)?
☐ Mail merge capability?

Database Management

☐ Basic search and sort functions?
☐ Specification of report formats?
☐ Relational capabilities (use common fields)?

Spreadsheets

☐ Basic calculation and formatting options?
☐ Scope of built-in functions?
☐ Graphing functions?

Graphics/Desktop Presentation

☐ Extent of graphs produced?
☐ Ability to create freehand drawings?
☐ Create slide shows?

Telecommunications

☐ Send and receive files and electronic mail?
☐ Access to online databases?
☐ Availability of computer conferences?

Integrated Software

☐ Easy transfer of data across programs?
☐ All applications work the same?

4

Computers in the Classroom

As we discussed in the introductory chapter, one of the major roles of any educational administrator is leadership. In the context of computers, this means motivating teachers and staff to use computers to improve their effectiveness and productivity in the classroom. It also includes helping teachers and staff make good decisions about classroom use and making sure that they are successful in whatever they choose to do.

This presents a dilemma for the administrator. In order to provide the leadership needed, a thorough understanding of computer applications in the classroom is required. However, given the spectrum of responsibilities of an administrator, an in-depth knowledge of classroom applications is not a very realistic expectation. Instead, the administrator should know what applications are possible, the benefits and limitations of each application, and the financial implications in terms of hardware, software, and support needed.[1]

APPLICATIONS PROGRAMS

Probably the single most important category of software for the classroom is the applications programs that you have already been

---

[1] For further discussion of computer applications in the classroom, see Bork (1985), Riesdesel and Clements (1985), or Snyder and Palmer (1988).

introduced to in the previous chapter. Because these programs are general purpose problem-solving tools, they are just as useful in teaching as in administration.

Consider word processing. It can be applied to all subjects since students have to write essays or reports in almost every class they take. Once a student has learned how to use a word processing program, it becomes a general computer skill they can use throughout their school experience and their career. Word processing also eliminates problems associated with illegible handwriting. In addition, there are many writing utility programs, such as spelling and grammar checkers, that can be used in conjunction with word processing to improve writing abilities. Such utilities are especially appropriate for use in Language Arts and English classes.[2]

Desktop publishing software and more sophisticated word processing programs can be used in many different classes to create newsletters, posters, reports, forms, and labels. Similarly, database management, spreadsheet, graphics, and telecommunications programs have general use across different curriculum areas.[3] Database management programs can be used for projects in history, geography, science, home economics, or health classes. The use of databases encourages the collection and analysis of facts and their interrelationships. Spreadsheets are especially useful in math, science, business, and athletics classes. They make it easier for students to analyze numerical data and reach conclusions. Graphics software can be used in a diverse range of classes, including art, drafting, finance, science, and math, to draw illustrations, produce schematics, create graphs, or plot data.[4]

Telecommunications programs can be used by students to exchange ideas or obtain information for projects in any area of study. The use of networks can eliminate geographical boundaries and allow students to interact with others of similar (or different) interests. Furthermore, networks can largely wash out many of the limitations experienced by handicapped students when they try to interact with other students. The use of networks is an important aspect of distance learning approaches (see Chapter 10).

---

[2] See Daiute (1985), Hertz (1986), or Wresch (1988) for more discussion about computers and writing.

[3] See Hunter (1984) for more details about the use of databases in the classroom.

[4] See Williams and LeCesne (1985) for a discussion of graphics software in the classroom.

There are many benefits in the use of applications software in the classroom. The use of these programs by students facilitates the development of higher order thinking skills, such as problem solving, decision making, and judgment. It also makes class assignments more interesting and challenging. Word processing and networks can improve the communication skills of students. In addition, the computer skills that students learn will be useful to them after they graduate and join the workforce.

The use of applications programs raises a number of issues and problems. First, students must be taught how to use the programs by someone. Not only does this take away valuable class time, but also causes disagreement about who should teach what. For example, if word processing is used primarily in English class, should it be taught in that class by the English teacher? Most schools recognize that computer skills should be taught by a computer specialist in a separate class, but not all schools have such a resource or can accommodate the class. Another important consideration is that students need a lot of computer time to use these tools. With the average computer-to-student ratio of 1 to 30, it is clear that there are not enough machines in most schools to make this a possibility on a large scale. Furthermore, in order to use these tools for their homework, they need access to machines at home. While this may be okay for affluent families, most students cannot count on having a computer at home to use.

From a financial perspective, applications software is a good investment because the same programs can be used across many curriculum areas and grade levels. Quantity discounts and site licenses are available for most programs. Integrated programs are especially good deals since they provide a set of applications for less than the price of the individual programs. From a teacher training perspective, applications software is advantageous because once a teacher has mastered a particular application, they can apply it across all teaching areas as well as administrative duties.

INSTRUCTIONAL SOFTWARE

A second category of software that may be useful in the classroom is programs specifically written to teach certain skills or subjects. These programs take the form of drills, tutorials, simulations, or games.

DOES COMPUTER-BASED
INSTRUCTION WORK?*

One of the enduring questions in the field of educational computing is: Do computers improve learning? The New York City Board of Education decided to investigate this question in the context of educationally disadvantaged students. In the 1987/88 school year, computer-based instruction systems from 13 different vendors were placed in 26 elementary and secondary schools throughout the city. The vendors provided the equipment, training, support, and maintenance, and the schools were responsible for providing staff. The Board of Education coordinated the project and conducted the evaluations.

Standardized reading and mathematics tests were used to measure achievement. The mid-1987 and 1988 scores of 1,734 students in reading and 1,351 students in math were compared. The results showed that almost all of the systems resulted in statistically significant gains in both reading and mathematics achievement. The overall gain in achievement was almost a full deviation score for both skill areas across all students and schools.

More detailed analysis of the data revealed some interesting trends. There was an inverse relationship between the student's instructional level and performance gains: The elementary students showed more gain than the high school students. It was also true that the more advanced students seem to benefit less from the use of the computer. Special education students showed the highest gains in achievement, followed by Chapter 1, bilingual, remedial, and general education. In other words, the type of computerized-based education provided by these systems (largely drills and tuto-

* Source: From "The Use of Computer-Based Instruction for the Basic Skills Remediation of Educationally Disadvantaged Students," by K. Swan et al., June 1989, *Proceedings, NECC 89*, Boston, MA.

rials on basic skills) helped the younger, most disadvantaged students the most.

When asked how learning via computers differed from their regular classroom activities, the students interviewed consistently said that they found computer learning less threatening. Students also stated that the opportunity to practice and the feedback they received while working on the computer was helpful. Teachers involved in the project felt that the diagnostic procedures used by the programs were the most valuable feature—both for the students and for themselves. Teachers reported that the computer freed them from their routine booking and disciplinary chores, and allowed them to spend more time with individual students.

The overall conclusion reached by the Board of Education from this study was that computer-based instruction can be effectively used to provide remedial instruction in reading and math to educationally disadvantaged inner-city students, particularly at lower levels of instruction. This conclusion is strongly supported by decades of research in the educational computing field.

There are thousands of such programs available for almost every aspect of the curriculum and grade level. Some software, such as SAT test preparation programs or keyboarding (typing) programs, are intended to help students with enabling skills rather than curriculum specific competencies.

Drills are programs that provide practice activities for students. They are most commonly used for building basic skills in arithmetic, spelling, or vocabulary (although they can be used for any subject area). Tutorials are programs that deliver full lessons on topics including practice exercises. Simulations are computer models of equipment, events, or processes that allow students to discover how things work in a particular domain. Games are similar to drills or simulations in nature, except they are designed to be entertaining.[5]

---

[5] Simulations are an extremely powerful and underused form of instructional software. (See Roberts, 1983, or Willis, Hovey, & Hovey, 1987.)

The major benefit of instructional software is that it provides individualized instruction. Students can proceed at their own pace and get feedback on their mistakes. The interactivity of the programs makes learning more interesting for most students. Furthermore, many instructional programs can collect student data and print out progress reports for the teacher to analyze. This data collection capability gives teachers the capability to diagnose students' problems in a more detailed fashion than is possible in traditional classes.

A long-standing question about instructional software is whether it really improves student learning. The evidence from many studies indicates that the use of instructional software can raise student achievement scores, although not consistently. One of the critical factors that determines whether a program will or will not be effective is how it is used by the teacher. In other words, if teachers are enthusiastic about a program, it is more likely to produce the desired results.[6]

Instructional software can be especially effective with students who have learning deficiencies or need remediation in basic skills. Such students often need more attention than other students which teachers cannot provide due to time limitations. Computer drills, tutorials, and games can help a teacher design learning activities that focus on the specific deficiency or limitations of the student. There are many programs designed for special education students.[7]

The major issue in the use of instructional software is in fitting it into the existing curriculum. If a teacher finds a program that is worthwhile and wants to use it in class, he or she must figure out how to integrate the computer activity into current teaching activities. The program can be used with the whole class as a group activity, it can be assigned to students to use in small groups, or it can be given as an individual activity for specific students. The location of computers in the school and policies for their use affects the options possible (see Chapter 6).

Another major issue is the time required to find and evaluate suitable instructional programs. This involves reading through catalogs

---

[6] See Jamison (1975), Kulick, Bangert, and Williams (1983), Niemiec and Walberg (1987), or Roblyer (1988) for summaries of effectiveness studies.

[7] See Budoff, Thorman, and Gras (1984), Goldenberg, Russell, and Carter (1984), Guilbeau (1984), or White (1984) for detailed discussion of computers in special education.

and magazines, using print or online directories, and talking to other teachers. Once a program is obtained, more time is required to learn how it works and to plan its use in the classroom. While the availability of computer specialists can significantly reduce the amount of time required to locate and use instructional software, the teacher still needs to be familiar with the program in order to integrate it into other classroom activities.[8]

Building a collection of instructional software for a school can be an expensive proposition. Different programs will be needed for each subject area and grade level, and more than one copy is likely to be needed. For example, imagine that each of five departments in a K–8 elementary school requested 10 programs. This is a total of 50 separate programs. Even if the programs have an average price of only $100 each, this amounts to $5,000. On the other hand, such a collection could significantly improve the quality of learning in the entire school, provided that the programs were well chosen and properly integrated into the curriculum.

PROGRAMMING LANGUAGES

In the early days of educational computing, there was a strong bias towards teaching all students how to program, especially using the BASIC programming language. The rationale was the students needed to understand how computers worked, and learning a programming language was the best way to do this.

The belief that most students should be taught how to program has been discarded by almost all computer educators. It is clear that learning how to use applications programs is more worthwhile to most students than learning how to program. While programming is an interesting and challenging activity, it does not seem relevant to the needs of most students unless they plan to pursue a career in the computer science field. Thus, the proper context for teaching how to program is as a college prep course or computer club activity.

There is one exception to this generalization: the LOGO programming language. LOGO is a simple but powerful language designed for young children (5–12 years old) to use as a vehicle for

---

[8] Lathrop and Goodson (1984) provide evaluation guidelines for selecting and using instructional software.

learning concepts in math, language, sciences, and music. Even though students learn to program, this is not the end in itself. Curriculums have been designed around LOGO, and there are also a number of related programs, such as LOGOWriter (a word processor for young children) and LOGO/LEGO, a set of programmable building components. In order to use LOGO in the classroom effectively, teachers need special training that can be obtained by attending workshops or special conference sessions.[8]

The same remarks made for students and programming can also be made for teachers and programming. In the early days of teacher training for computers, it was felt to be important for teachers to be able to program. In addition to the rationale that it would help teachers understand computers, it was felt that teachers should be able to create their own programs. With the emergence of applications software and abundance of instructional programs, this rationale withered away. Furthermore, the presence of powerful authoring systems (Apple's HyperCard is probably the best known) has made it easier for teachers to create their own computer materials without learning to program.

MULTIMEDIA

Great progress has been made in the past decade in the area of computer-controlled video and audio. Computer interaction does not need to be limited to viewing text or graphic displays. Students can watch photographs and video sequences, talk to the computer and have it talk back, and use it to synthesize music.

Videodiscs and CD-ROMS provide photographic and video collections that can be accessed via computer and displayed on the computer screen. There are many videodisc-based instructional programs available in areas such as science, foreign languages, history, geography, and art appreciation. These programs can be used by the teacher with the whole class, or for small group and individual use. While current CD-ROMs don't have the same capacity as the larger videodiscs, they are more convenient to use.

The primary benefit of using videodiscs and CD-ROM is that they provide a way to include photographic and video sequences in

[9] For more about LOGO, see Papert (1980) or Watt and Watt (1986).

interactive instruction. For example, a standard videodisc can hold over 50,000 photographs! The Grolier Electronic Encyclopedia consists of 31 volumes of information on a single CD-ROM disc. From a learning perspective, they provide a way of making a lesson more interesting and stimulating.

Instructional programs can also take advantage of speech input and synthesis. The program can recognize words and phrases spoken by the student and match them to correct responses. The program can also pronounce words and phrases. A number of programs for language arts and reading make use of speech input/output capabilities. Spoken output is also important in programs designed for the blind.

Finally, there is a large collection of software available for music composition and instruction. These programs allow students to compose music without the need for instruments, as well as provide instruction in music theory and composition. Such programs would allow a music department of offer a greater range of learning activities with fewer actual instruments.

The main concern with multimedia applications is that additional equipment and software is needed. However, this equipment and software can be shared by a department or entire school. There is also only a limited amount of material available in videodisc and CD-ROM format. Therefore, multimedia systems should only be purchased on the basis of a well-planned proposal that describes what materials will be used and how. Of course, this is good advice for the acquisition of any software or hardware (see Chapter 5).

TEACHER UTILITIES AND STUDENT MANAGEMENT PROGRAMS

A considerable portion of a teacher's time is spent making up and grading tests, keeping track of grades, scheduling student activities, creating and revising lesson plans, and writing reports or proposals. Time saved on these administrative duties could be channeled into teaching and student activities. The use of applications software, as well as some of the specialized administrative programs discussed in Chapter 2, can help teachers reduce the amount of time devoted to nonteaching tasks.

One of the major concerns in providing teachers with help for their administrative activities is coordination. If each teacher uses a different program for test scoring or writing proposals, the capability to share their expertise or data with each other or the office is reduced. Programs may not work on all machines or the data files created may be incompatible. Thus, it is in the school's best interest if all teachers use the same programs. To make sure this happens, someone has to assess teacher needs, select software that meets these needs, and provide the necessary training.

The need for some form of student management software becomes critical if an attempt is made to track the progress of each student individually, as is the case in competency-based or special education programs. Because of the frequency of tests and the need to regularly print progress charts, computerized testing and report generation are almost essential. However, computer-managed instruction is a major undertaking for a school or district and requires a lot of planning and special expertise.[10]

SUMMARY

There are many ways to use computers in the classroom. Applications software can be used in many different subject areas and grade levels. Instructional programs include drills, tutorials, simulations and games; they are usually specific to a particular subject and grade level. The LOGO programming language can be used in elementary grades to teach concepts in math, language, science, and music. Videodisc and CD-ROM materials can be used in a variety of subjects to present computer-controlled multimedia lessons. Utility programs are available to help teachers create tests, keep grades, make up schedules, and prepare budgets.

Each different approach to using computers in the classroom has it's own special considerations. One problem that applies to all approaches is the amount of time required to prepare computer-based activities. Teachers must know the software well enough to teach with it and help students when they have difficulties. They also must figure out how to integrate the computer activities into the

---

[10] See Baker (1978) or Goodson (1984) for further discussion of computer-managed instruction.

existing curriculum and other teaching activities. In the case of instructional software and multimedia materials, additional time is required to find suitable programs and to evaluate them. Clearly, teachers need some form of release time and access to computers in order to prepare computer activities.

The majority of teachers are likely to be enthusiastic about the use of computers in the classroom. For these teachers, your task as an administrator is to make sure they have the resources (hardware, software, facilities) needed. This task is made easier through proper planning that includes teacher involvement (see next chapter). Some teachers will be indifferent or antagonistic towards the use of computers. You need to provide these teachers with additional exposure to the potential of computers through attendance at workshops and conferences, or by working with a computer specialist in their subject area. Of course, not every teacher needs to use computers in their classroom. This is another important aspect of your task as technology leader—to make decisions about which computer applications are most worthwhile. Chapter 8 tries to provide some guidelines for making such decisions.

EXERCISES

1. By talking to teachers or computer specialists in your school or school district, make a list of instructional programs that they currently use or would like to have. Find out how they integrate the programs into their existing classroom activities. Ask them to estimate how long it would take to learn to use the programs.
2. If you were to make an integrated program available to all teachers and students in your school, what applications would they use for what learning activities? Who would show teachers and students how to use the program? Would there be enough machines for the uses envisioned?
3. Examine some of the software available for some aspect of special education or remedial learning activities in a school. Ask the teachers or students involved if they feel this software would be useful to them. Find out why/why not.
4. Imagine that you have a budget that limits you to acquiring software for only one subject area in a school or school district. What subject would you pick and why?

5. A teacher comes to you with a request to buy a videodisc program. What questions would you ask before you approve the request?

CHECKLIST FOR CLASSROOM SOFTWARE

Application Programs

☐ Who is going to teach students to use programs?
☐ Are there enough computers for all students?
☐ Do you want to emphasize higher order thinking skills?

Instructional Software

☐ Is individualized instruction important?
☐ Are teachers enthusiastic about software?
☐ Can this software be used for students with special needs?
☐ Will teachers be able to integrate programs into existing curricula?
☐ Who will evaluate and select software?

Programming Languages

☐ Is too much emphasis placed on programming activities?
☐ Would LOGO be helpful for some students?
☐ Do teachers have the time/background to create software?

Multimedia

☐ Would videodiscs or CD-ROM be useful?
☐ Would speech input/output have benefits to some students?
☐ Would music software be useful?

Teacher Utilities

☐ Would utility software save teachers time?
☐ Are utility programs compatible with other administrative software being used?
☐ Would a computer-managed instruction system be worthwhile?

5

Evaluating Hardware and Software Alternatives

One of the anomalies of using computers is that the two major components (hardware and software) do not usually play a critical role in the success of computer applications. This is because implementation factors (to be discussed in the next chapter) typically overshadow the importance of the particular hardware and software involved. On the other hand, there are some situations where the selection of the right computer system can make the difference between success or failure. In any event, something must be selected since there can be no computing activities without hardware and software.

This chapter discusses the hardware and software alternatives possible. It also provides guidelines for evaluating hardware and software.

HARDWARE ALTERNATIVES

There are a bewildering number of hardware choices possible, and new developments seem to appear every week. The major components of a computer system are described below along with a discussion of characteristics or options that are important in selection or evaluation considerations.

CPUs

The Central Processing Unit (CPU) defines the type and capabilities of the computer. A major distinction is made on the basis of the CPU size: mainframe computers versus minicomputers versus desktop systems. Mainframe computers are typically room size; minicomputers are about the size of a desk; and desktop computers resemble typewriters with display screens. Laptop computers are the newest type of system—they are about the size of a telephone book. As a general rule, the larger the computer, the more processing power and storage space available. Furthermore, the larger the computer system, the more suitable the computer is for networking.

The most important characteristics of the CPU is probably the amount of RAM (Random Access Memory) available. The amount of RAM determines how large a program or file (or how many) can be processed at one time. The more RAM available, the faster the computer can work, especially if complex programs or large data files are involved. Most personal computers have 1–2 megabytes (million bytes) of RAM, whereas minicomputers and mainframes have hundreds of megabytes of RAM. For administrative applications in a single school, the amount of RAM on a personal computer is adequate; however, to process data from many schools, the larger RAM found in a minicomputer or mainframe is usually needed.

Each different brand or model of computer uses different microprocessor chips and proprietary circuit boards. The situation is much like automobiles with different engines and transmissions; they all have similar parts and function the same way, but the details are different. In the personal computer realm, there are currently four dominant types of machines used in schools: the Apple II, the Apple Macintosh, the IBM PC, and the IBM PS/2. The Apple II and IBM PC are older machines that have been around for some years; the Macintosh and the PS/2 are more recent machines with more capabilities.

Display Capabilities

One of the more important characteristics of a computer system is the kind of display capabilities possible. In order to display graphics or different type styles, as well as color on the screen, it is necessary to have a display monitor capable of graphics. Older computer systems (especially mainframes) used terminals that were only capable of monochrome (single color) text display. Most modern personal computers are capable of color graphics, although the type of graphics and the number of colors possible varies across systems.

Screen resolution is a significant factor in determining the type of graphics possible. The higher the resolution, the more detail that can be displayed. Resolution is measured in pixels (an abbreviation for picture elements) which are the individually addressable points on the screen. If a screen can display 500 rows x 500 columns, it would have a resolution of 250,000 pixels. This is about the resolution of most personal computer displays in use today. Newer computers are likely to have displays with resolutions of one million pixels (1,000 x 1,000).

Since most instructional applications of computers require high quality graphics and color, resolution is an important selection factor. While most administrative applications deal with words and numbers, there is an increasing need for graphics capability in applications such as desktop publishing and presentations. Furthermore, the desire for improved legibility and more information on a screen leads to a need for higher resolution displays. In particular, the use of windowing capabilities in programs to allow multiple views of information on the same screen requires high-resolution displays.

Ergonomics is another important consideration for displays. Screen displays should tilt and swivel so the user can adjust the viewing angle to suit their personal preference. If this is not a feature of the computer, movable display stands can be bought that provide such adjustment capabilities. Another ergonomic consideration is non-glare screens that do not reflect light and make the screen difficult to read. Again, these can be bought separately and attached to the displays. If staff and students are going to spend a lot of time viewing computer screens, such ergonomic measures are worthwhile.

Disk Drives

Another important aspect of a computer system is the type of disk storage available. Programs and data are stored on disk when not being actively used. Disk storage is measured in thousands of bytes where the letter "K" represents one thousand bytes. A single character takes about 1 byte to store, so a 2,000 word document consisting of 10,000 characters would require about 10K bytes to store.

Floppy disks are the most common form of storage. Two sizes of floppy disks are in use—the older 5¼ inch disks and the newer 3½ disks. In an irony typical of the computing field, the smaller disks have more than twice the capacity as the older larger disks (approximately 800K bytes). There are also high-density floppy disks that hold even more.

Hard disks have much higher storage capacity than floppy disks, but cannot be removed from the computer. The smallest hard disks on personal computers hold 20–40 megabytes, and the larger hard disks found in mainframe systems hold 400–500 megabytes of data. Most computer systems have a combination of floppy and hard disk drives. The floppy disks are used to store information that may need to be used on more than one machine as well as backup copies of files, while hard disks are used to store programs and data that are used routinely on the same machine.

Printers

Since the end result of many administrative applications is a printed document or report, the kind of printing capabilities provided by a computer system are important. The two key factors in evaluating printers are quality and speed. The most common type of printer in use today is a dot-matrix printer. Dot-matrix printers are relatively inexpensive, can produce so-called "letter quality" output, and can print reasonably fast (1–2 pages per minute).

Faster and better quality output is produced by a laser printer. Although laser printers are considerably more expensive than dot-matrix printers, the output looks like typeset quality, and they can print 6–8 pages per minute. For word processing and desktop publishing applications, this quality and speed are highly desirable.

Because of their cost, laser printers are usually shared by a number of computers in a local area network.

There are lots of other types of printers other than these two. Thermal printers are inexpensive and small but require special paper. Ink jet printers are very quiet and can do color. Plotters are used in engineering and architectural applications to print large detailed specifications in multiple colors. You may also run into older "daisy wheel" and line printers in some offices and data processing departments. Apart from special applications, dot-matrix and laser printers constitute the two major choices.

Input Devices

There are a number of different ways to get information into a computer. The standard method is via the keyboard. Most of the newer personal computers use a mouse for selecting options on the screen. For certain applications, such as graphics or desktop publishing, a mouse is very important since a lot of screen movement is involved. A graphics tablet is another way of manipulating information on the screen and is very popular in computer-aided design (CAD) applications.

Besides the keyboard, the most important input device for administrative applications is the OCR (Optical Character Reader) scanner. A scanner can read the information on a printed page or card and convert it into electronic form. An OCR is designed to read just checkmarks, but other types of scanners (sometimes called "digitizers") can convert illustrations or printed text. OCR scanners are widely used in schools to read attendance sheets, registration cards, test answer forms, questionnaire responses, and employee time cards.

While we do not see many examples in school applications, input can also be done by touch and voice. Touch screens are available for many computers that allow people to make choices by touching options on the screen. Touch input is popular in computers used for exhibits and kiosks in public places, such as museums, airports, shopping plazas, and so on. Voice input is used for special applications, such as language learning and reading or with visually impaired individuals. It is possible that we will see much greater use of these two input modes in future computers; at the present time they are not as flexible or reliable as the standard keyboard method.

You should also be aware of the many special input devices designed for the physically handicapped. This includes special keyboards with enlarged keys and joysticks that can be used to control cursor movement.

Video Projectors and LCD Panels

One category of equipment that is especially important to education are devices that allow the display screen to be projected on a wall for group viewing. In order for teachers to be able to use the computer with their whole class, or for administrators to be able to show computer slides in a meeting, such a device is critical.

There are two types of devices currently available for projecting screens: video projectors and LCD panels. Video projectors are large units that are usually built into a podium or the ceiling; LCD tablets are small and less expensive units that must be used in conjunction with an overhead projector. In addition to costing less, the LCD tablets are more portable and can be easily taken on trips.

An alternative to video projectors or LCD panels is to use a video camera focused on the display and a series of large video monitors (e.g., 19 or 25 inch). This works for small groups of 6–10 people, but does not produce the legibility of a projected image. For this reason, it is recommended that every school using computers have at least one video projector or LCD panel. To facilitate group presentations on a regular basis, a number of these devices will be needed.

Modems

Although they are a somewhat specialized piece of hardware, modems are needed by any computer that is going to be used for telecommunications. As telecommunications becomes an increasingly common use of computers, modems will come to be considered a standard computer system component.

As you have probably come to expect at this point, modems come in a variety of different types. Most modems are slim rectangular boxes that connect to the serial interface at the back of the computer and also plug into a standard phone jack. However, modems can also be located inside the computer on a circuit card. In this case, the phone jack plugs directly into the back of the computer. There are also "pocket modems" that are about the size of a cigarette pack and battery powered. Designed specifically for traveling and use with laptops, they usually plug directly into the serial connector on the back of the computer.

The most important selection criteria for modems is their speed. Modems can transmit/receive at different speeds measured in characters per second (cps) or baud rate (1 cps = 1 baud). The most common speed in use today is 1,200 baud, although older modems may transmit at 300 baud, and new modems may support 2,400 baud or higher. Many modems support a range of speeds from 300 to 2,400, which can be selected by the communications program used. As a general rule, a single-speed modem is less expensive than one that supports a range of speeds.

Summary

When selecting computer hardware, decisions about the major components (CPU, displays, printers, input devices, and modems) will need to made. Each component comes in a variety of different types with different capabilities. Which capabilities are desired will be dictated by the specific needs of the application, cost limitations, and compatibility considerations.

SOFTWARE ALTERNATIVES

Just as it is necessary to make choices about hardware alternatives, it is also essential to make selections among different software alternatives. To do this, you need to be familiar with the various types of software possible. In many cases, the choice of particular software will dictate corresponding hardware choices.

Operating Systems

An operating system is the program that manages the input, output, and processing of the computer. It takes care of getting the computer started when you turn it on. It allows you to read from, and write files to, the disk. The operating system also allows you to make copies and delete files, print, and control the screen. Some operating systems also include capabilities to communicate with other computers in a network.

Each major type of computer tends to have its own unique operating system. For example, Apple IIs, Apple Macintoshes, IBM PCs, and IBM PS/2s all have different operating systems which are incompatible with each other (although the DOS operating system used by the IBM PC can also run on PS/2 systems, and there is some degree of transfer between the Apple IIGS and the Macintosh). Since the operating systems are incompatible, they cannot run the same software. Most minicomputer systems and some mainframes use the UNIX operating system originally developed by Bell Labs. Unlike the operating systems found on personal computers, UNIX runs on many different computers, although there are a number of different versions which are not totally compatible. Most mainframes tend to use operating systems initially developed by IBM (even though they may not be IBM computers).

The various operating systems differ in their ease of use and their capabilities. For example, the operating system of the Apple II is quite limited relative to those found on other personal computers. The operating system of the Apple Macintosh is visually-oriented and very easy to use. Both the DOS and UNIX operating systems involve learning hundreds of commands, and hence, are not well-suited to casual use. The operating systems found in mainframe systems are quite complex and usually require a trained computer operator. On the other hand, there is a general trend towards the development of easy-to-use operating systems for all levels of systems. For example, the new operating systems for IBM PS/2 machines (called OS/2 or PS/2), as well as for UNIX-based computers, are major improvements over earlier software.

Since operating systems normally come with the computer, they are not something that can be decided upon independently of the hardware system. However, it is conceivable that a computer could be selected because it runs a certain operating system. For example, if you wanted to use a particular administrative system that only works with DOS, you would have no choice but to buy a PC or PS/2 machine. Similarly, if you were primarily concerned with selecting a computer system that required minimal training, you might select a Macintosh because of its easy-to-use operating system.

Applications Software

We have already discussed the nature of applications programs in detail in previous chapters. It is important to understand that such programs are designed for specific operating systems, and hence, can only run on the machine they are designed for. Some of the more popular programs have versions for different machines which are similar but not identical. For example, you might decide that you want to buy a specific word processing program that is available for both the IBM PC and Apple II. The two versions would come on separate disks for each machine. However, the program would look and work the same way on the two machines, and if you knew how to use it on one machine, you would be able to use it on the other, provided you knew how to use both operating systems.

If a program only runs on one type of machine, you will have to decide if it is important enough to determine the type of hardware selected. If you have already made your hardware selection or have existing equipment, you can narrow down your evaluation of software to those programs that run on it. For this reason, many experts recommend that you select the software you want to use first before making decisions about hardware. In the long run, software capabilities are likely to be much more important than hardware features.

Selection of an applications program can be a difficult task. You must spend enough time learning a program to determine if you like it and if it meets your needs. On the other hand, if you are comparing a number of different programs, you can't spend a lot of time looking at each one. The best way to evaluate an applications program is to have an experienced user show you how it handles the kinds of tasks you expect to use it for. It is always difficult to be sure a program will do exactly what you want until after you have used it for a while.

Probably the most important selection criterion for applications programs is to pick software that has the right degree of power and usability. All applications software comes in a range from very simple and easy to very sophisticated and complex. The low-end programs are inexpensive and take little time to learn, but they also have only the basic features. The high-end programs tend to be more expensive, have many features, and take much longer to learn. You need to decide which end of the spectrum you want to be on. It is not unusual to pick two programs for each application, one low-end program for beginners or casual users and the other a high-end program for heavy duty users. Of course, it is important that both programs can share the same files so that people can exchange data and migrate from one program to the other.

Administrative Software

In Chapter 2, we discussed the many types of administrative programs available. Unlike applications software where the same program may exist for more than one system or where a full range of choices exist for each different computer, administrative software tends to be much more unique and tailored to a specific computer system. Not only may the program only work on a specific computer, but it may also require a particular type of printer, memory size, or input device (e.g., OCR scanner).

An important selection factor for administrative programs is the amount of flexibility they provide. Since they cannot be easily changed like applications programs, administrative programs need to have a lot of configuration options. You should be able to specify report layouts, field lengths, screen displays, and input formats. Without such flexibility, the use of a program will be limited and may not result in as much productivity improvement as possible.

Instructional Software

The primary selection considerations for instructional software should be curriculum or teaching requirements. It should meet explicit instructional objectives, cover the appropriate grade/age levels, or be backed up by some form of effectiveness data. Instructional programs should be well documented, including both student and teacher guides as well as having ample online helps. Above all, instructional software should be selected by the teachers who are going to use the programs. Despite state-mandated curriculums, classroom teaching is still very much an individual matter, and teachers must be comfortable with a particular program in order for them to teach with it.

One important consideration for most instructional programs is extensibility. Extensibility refers to the capability to add or replace data sets and possibly add custom data. For example, a teacher should be able to replace problems or questions with their own or add their own feedback messages. This allows them to adapt the program to their own classroom or student needs, as well as add new material when students get bored with what is provided. Programs that allow teachers to specify their own teaching styles or strategies are especially desirable.

A special problem in acquiring any software for student use (this would include applications programs as well as instructional software) is obtaining multiple copies or site licensing. It is tempting to students and teachers to buy a single copy of a program and then make as many copies as needed. This is an area where educational administrators must be vigilant to promote and enforce copyright laws. Every school should have a written policy on adherence to copyright law that is posted in every classroom or lab where computers are located. Severe disciplinary action should be taken against any students or staff who violate copyright policies. Not only is this an important ethical issue, but it can be financially disastrous for a school or individual involved in a copyright lawsuit.[1]

Programming Languages and Authoring Systems

Earlier in this book, we warned about the unnecessary teaching of programming based upon historical precedents that no longer apply. Our point was that programming is a valid subject for computer science students, but not very relevant to people who simply use a computer. Given the plethora of software that now exists, there is little reason for anyone to have to write their own program, and hence, learn a programming language. From this it follows that selection of programming software should be left to computer science teachers for use in their teaching.

Authoring systems represent a slightly different situation, although you should still exercise a good deal of caution before purchasing this kind of software. Authoring systems make it possible to create instructional programs without the need for any programming. The designer specifies the screens and program flow and the authoring system automatically constructs a working program from these specifications. However, even though there is no programming re-

---

[1] See Brady (1985) for a description of what happens when schools fail to do this.

quired. The development of good instructional programs is a very time-consuming activity—tantamount to the effort involved in writing a textbook or making a professional quality video or film. For this reason it is important to be sure that there is no existing instructional software that could be used, that the developer has the necessary time available, and that the resulting software will be used and worth the effort. Teachers should be able to create instructional programs when they really want to, but this decision should be subjected to some scrutiny in terms of having adequately researched existing software and the level of effort involved.[2]

As far as selection of the actual authoring system to be used is concerned, the most important consideration is probably the level of support available and the number of existing users. Typically, the development of a program involves a lot of problem solving, and advice from experts or people who know the authoring system well is highly desirable. Systems that have extensive documentation and sample programs are likely to be much easier to work with than those that provide little documentation, despite the number of features they offer. The same remarks hold true for the selection of programming languages as well.

Summary

While different selection factors are more or less important for each type of software, we can summarize a set of factors that should be considered when evaluating any software alternative. These factors include:

- usability—how easy is it to learn and use the program (how long does it take)?
- flexibility—how easily can the program parameters be changed?
- extensibility—can the program handle new data sets or new hardware options?
- support—is technical assistance available when needed?
- documentation—how comprehensive is it?

---

[2] See Allesi and Trollip (1985), Hannifin and Peck (1988), or Kearsley (1986) for details.

Software that rates highly on all of these factors is likely to work well; software that fails on one or more of these factors is likely to prove unsatisfactory.

INTEGRATED LEARNING SYSTEMS

When selecting hardware and software, there is one other major consideration that you should be aware of. A number of companies (e.g., CCC, Jostens, Wasatch, Wicat) market Integrated Learning Systems (ILSs) that consist of networked personal computers complete with instructional and student management software. The software resides on a hard disk (or in one case, CD-ROM) hence, the use of floppy disks is largely eliminated. The instructional software provided usually covers the major curriculum areas (such as language arts, math, social studies, physical sciences) as well as many grade levels. The student management software includes lesson tests, automatic test scoring, and a variety of student progress reports.

Integrated Learning Systems provide a simplified solution to the problems associated with selecting hardware and software. An ILS vendor provides a total "package" consisting of computers, software, teacher/staff training, and support. In most cases, the curriculum provided with the ILS has been through extensive evaluation at other school systems, and the system is thoroughly tested and reliable. The ILS vendor takes care of installation and maintenance, software updates, and trouble-shooting problems.

Despite its alluring benefits, there are a few drawbacks to the ILS approach. The cost of purchasing such a system is high—the price includes all the hardware and software components that would normally be bought separately. Many school systems cannot afford (or are unwilling) to spend so much on computer-based instruction in one lump sum. Another potential problem area is the nature of the curriculum provided. Even though the programs are usually well validated, they may not be the programs that your teachers want to use. While some of the ILS vendors offer some flexibility in this aspect by including desired programs to be added to the collection, their major focus tends to be on the curriculum they provide.

Integrated learning systems are probably a good choice for a school that wants to get involved in computer-based instruction with minimal effort. Such systems have proved to be effective solutions to specific instructional situations, such as remedial learning labs. They also provide a good way to establish a networked system in a school as a basis for other applications, such as administrative or library programs.

CONCLUSIONS

Evaluating hardware and software alternatives is a complex decision process that involves many different considerations. In selecting hardware, you need to determine what capabilities are needed for the particular applications planned. For example, if the computers are to be used for any type of financial or student database applications, a lot of storage is likely to be needed, and hence, a hard disk is essential. If the computer system is to be used for desktop publishing, a laser printer and mouse will be needed. If the computers are being purchased primarily for instructional applications, color graphics displays will probably be required. Different hardware is likely to be needed for different purposes in the school. Without a firm grasp of what the computer is going to be used for, it is very difficult to make good hardware decisions.

When selecting software, you must take into account who will be using the programs. The level of computer experience, the amount of training likely, and the extent of use are all factors to be taken into account to determine the appropriate levels of useability, flexibility, and support required. Software purchased for use by teachers will have different characteristics than programs bought for use by front office staff. Certain individuals will prefer the way one program works over another. Regardless of the program features, people must like a program if they are to use it extensively.

While we discussed hardware and software selection separately, they are highly interdependent activities. In buying any hardware and software, compatibility is a major concern. Since not all programs work with all types of hardware, it is critical to check this out before final purchase arrangements are made. In many cases, compatibility cannot be assured until all hardware and software are actually together and running. For this reason, vendors should be required to demonstrate compatibility before the sale is completed.

Integrated Learning Systems provide a simplified alternative for selecting hardware and software since these systems come as a complete "package." However, an ILS does not address the full scope of applications we have discussed in earlier chapters, and hence, are best considered solutions to specific aspects of school computer needs. In any event, all of the selection criteria discussed in this chapter still need to be applied in the selection of a particular ILS.

Chapter 8 discusses the cost/benefits of computer use and provides some additional considerations to be taken into account when selecting a computer system. In addition, the next chapter on implementation covers some topics that have implications for evaluating hardware and software.

EXERCISES

1. Imagine that you have just been assigned to a new school that has no computers. How would you go about determining what hardware and software to acquire?
2. For a school that already has computers, make a list of the additional hardware and software desired. What factors should be taken into account in selecting the particular hardware and software?
3. Develop a checklist or evaluation form to be used in selecting hardware or software.
4. Pick one category of hardware or software and conduct a selection study for your school. Be sure to explain the rationale for the selection made.
5. Do you think it is easier to select hardware or software? Why? What are the similarities and differences in selecting hardware versus software?
6. Compare the hardware or software selections of two different schools. How did the selection process differ? Do you think that one school made better selections than the other?

CHECKLIST FOR HARDWARE/SOFTWARE

Hardware Alternatives

- [ ] How much memory (RAM) is needed for the CPU?
- [ ] Is color graphics capability needed?
- [ ] What screen resolution is needed?
- [ ] How important are ergonomic considerations?
- [ ] What kind of disk drives are needed?
- [ ] What kind of printers are needed?
- [ ] Are mice needed?
- [ ] Is an OCR scanner needed?
- [ ] How many LCD panels or video projectors are needed?
- [ ] How many modems are needed?

Software Alternatives

- [ ] Is a particular operating system needed?
- [ ] Will the software desired run under the operating system available?
- [ ] Does the software match the degree of simplicity or sophistication needed?
- [ ] Is the software easy to use?
- [ ] Is the software flexible enough to accomodate changes needed?
- [ ] Does instructional software meet the curriculum needs?
- [ ] Can instructional software be customized to the needs of teachers?
- [ ] Does authoring software have good support and a large user community?

Integrated Learning Systems

- [ ] Can additional student stations and peripherals be added to the network?
- [ ] Can additional software be added to the network?
- [ ] Does the student management software provide the reports desired?

6

Successful Computer Implementation

This chapter discusses factors that affect the successful implementation of computers in schools, including facilities, staffing, training, security, and maintenance. While many of these aspects are mundane, experience has shown that they are the factors that can make the difference between failure and success. Selecting the right hardware or software does not guarantee success if poor implementation decisions are made.

FACILITIES

Of all the implementation decisions that must be made, the location of computers is probably the most difficult and potentially ruinous. Where the computers are located largely dictates how they will be used and by whom.

For administrative applications, computers can be located in people's offices or in a shared work area. There are pros and cons to both arrangements. Putting the computer in a person's office makes the machine easily available and increases the chances it will be used often. The extra effort involved in going to another office to use the computer is often enough of a nuisance to prevent its use. On the other hand, putting a computer in a public area usually results in much better utilization of machines, and also prevents them from becoming "status symbols" and expensive decorations.

A similar situation exists for instructional applications. Computers can be located in classrooms or in labs where their use is scheduled. Putting computers in the classroom makes it easier for teachers to integrate them into the curriculum since they are always available. However, they may sit idle much of the time. If located in a lab they can be utilized more. Furthermore, a computer coordinator or lab assistant who is knowledgeable about the hardware and software used can be available at all times. When the computers are located in the classroom, teachers must provide all assistance.[1]

A more subtle aspect of the location issue is which students get access to computers. For example, if computers are put in a science or math classroom, but not in a language arts or social studies classroom, there is a bias towards students who take math or science in terms of computer access. Putting computers in a lab theoretically makes access equal. Along these lines, computers are sometimes located in the library to facilitate equal access. However, there are problems with locating computers in the library, such as conflicts between quiet reading areas and sometimes noisy computer usage.

In many cases, shared computers are an economic necessity. There are not enough computers to locate them in individual offices or classrooms. Putting this aside for the moment, which location is most desirable? Experience suggests that both alternatives have their merits in certain situations, and the best plan is to have computers in offices and classrooms, as well as shared areas and labs. For some administrators and teachers who use computers extensively, the machines should be located in their office or classroom. Other staff and teachers will be quite satisfied with using machines in public areas and labs as needed. Thus, the ideal approach is to set up clusters of machines in open areas and labs while locating machines in the offices and classrooms of any staff member or teacher who indicates a legitimate need.

There is one other possible solution to the location problem. This is to have machines on mobile carts so they can be moved around the school as needed. This approach makes sense for systems that have special characteristics (such as videodisc or CD-ROM players),

---

[1] See Fisher and Finkel (1984) for a summary of the pros and cons of the lab approach.

but could lead to a scheduling and logistics nightmare if employed on a large scale.

Beyond the issue of where the computers will be located, there are other facilities considerations. These include:

- furnishings—computers, disk drives, and printers all need suitable furniture—especially ample desk or table space to accommodate books, notepads, and software documentation.
- storage areas—software and documentation, as well as computer supplies, spare hardware, and shipping boxes all need to be kept somewhere. A large storage area is essential.
- power outlets—computers and peripherals use up a lot of power outlets. Furthermore, the power needs to be reliable.
- air conditioning—computers tend to generate a lot of heat; more than two or three in a room will necessitate air conditioning.

As should be clear, making decisions about computer facilities takes a good deal of planning and consultation with many members of a school staff.[2]

STAFFING

Of equal importance in successful implementation is proper staffing. Special expertise is needed to ensure that computers are used effectively in a school. This includes initial and ongoing help from computer specialists for both administrative and classroom applications.

Most school districts and many larger schools have a permanent computer coordinator on their staff. The job responsibilities of the computer coordinator include:

- assisting teachers and staff in evaluating and selecting hardware and software
- teaching teachers and staff how to use existing computers and software
- conducting needs assessments to determine what additional computing resources might be desirable

---

[2] See Hill (1988) for further discussion of facilities planning.

- assisting teachers, staff, and students with problems using hardware or software
- supervising computer facilities, ordering supplies, and maintaining hardware/software
- interfacing with computer vendors and service personnel
- providing computer demonstrations to interested parents, board members, or visitors
- collaborating with teachers and staff in preparing computer budgets, reports, and proposals.

In large school districts, it is not unusual to have a district-level computer coordinator who supervises coordinators at each school.

As the number of computers in a school and district increases, managing these resources becomes a major activity. Without a computer coordinator, the tasks listed above must be handled by existing staff or teachers in addition to their regular duties. Under these circumstances, computer use in a school or school system is likely to be poorly managed due to lack of time or proper background. Computer coordinators usually have formal training in computing and considerable experience working with computers.

A second level of computer support that is highly desirable is one or more computer assistants or aides. Assistants perform duties, such as:

- showing students how to use programs or hardware and helping with any problems they have
- helping staff with data entry, OCR scanning, or printing
- helping teachers or coordinators set up equipment, prepare computer activities, or maintain software libraries
- helping to maintain hardware and software by replacing printer ribbons, and cleaning equipment.

A library or media specialist can also play an important role in computer support. This individual can catalog all instructional software and advise teachers on its suitability for their use in certain lessons, as well as link it to other materials (e.g., print, video) that may be available. To the extent that online databases or telecommunications activities are available, the library/media specialist can support these applications. Similarly, if a collection of videodiscs or CD-ROMs are available, the librarian/media specialist can help students/teachers use these resources.

In addition to these staff members, it is very likely that the assistance of computer consultants will be needed from time to time, especially when a new application is tried. For example, a desktop publishing expert should be consulted for advice on what system to purchase and to help conduct the initial training of staff who will use the system. Similarly, if a new classroom application is introduced, such as LOGO, IBM's Writing to Read, Apple's Early Learning series, videodisc/DC-ROM, or telecommunications, an expert in the application should be brought in to provide teachers with the proper orientation and initial training.

Even though a school may have a computer coordinator, it is not reasonable to expect this person to be an expert on all computer applications. Hiring a consultant allows a school to benefit from the experience of this individual in a specific application or area. If that experience helps staff or teachers get started faster on a new application and prevents some mistakes, the money spent on the consultant is probably well worth it. Consultants are also very useful in conducting feasibility or selection studies—not only do they have broader computer expertise, but they also are more objective and neutral with respect to internal school biases.

Without the necessary staff to supervise computer use, train teachers and other staff how to use computers, and ensure that the hardware and software are functional, computer activities are not likely to run very smoothly in a school or school system, if they run at all. When it comes to budgeting for computers in schools, it is essential that adequate funds be allocated for staff as well as for hardware and software.

TRAINING

Assuming that the proper facilities and staff are available for computers, the next major implementation concern is training. Without adequate training, it is unlikely that staff or teachers will learn how to use the computers and software available to the fullest extent possible. Even individuals who have computer experience need comprehensive training in order to learn a new application. While

GETTING TEACHERS INVOLVED WITH COMPUTERS*

How do you get teachers involved with computers? Finding an answer to this question is one of the major elements of a successful computer implementation strategy. Here are some ideas from two different school systems. Lake Washington school district, just outside Seattle, WA, rewards teachers with their own computer (an Apple IIGS) in exchange for their participation in computer in-service training. By attending nine days of training, teachers "earn" their own computer. For an additional two and a half days training, they can also qualify for a printer. When the program was first offered in the summer of 1987, 983 of the 1,050 teachers in the school district earned their own computers!

The training was conducted by a group of 36 teachers who had been trained earlier. The idea to use these teachers as trainers was initially motivated by cost considerations, but has had many benefits. Because these teachers are part of the system, they serve as an ongoing resources. In addition, they developed important leadership qualities which went beyond the computer training they provided.

How well did the teacher training work? In the second year following the summer training, the district received a flood of requests for software, peripherals, and additional training; computer user groups were organized by teachers; and computer newsletters created by teachers and students appeared. The availability of the computer training program serves as a valuable recruiting item to attract new teachers to the district. And, the program seems to have gotten the interest of the community—a $10 million bond was passed to buy new electronic equipment and upgrade schools to house new technology centers.

Across the country, in the Chittenden South School District in Shelburne, VT, another approach is used. In addition

* Source: The Electronic School, National School Boards Association, September 1988.

> to in-service computer courses (of which 90 percent of all teachers in the system have taken), the district provides small grants for projects that teachers propose. Each fall, teachers receive a packet containing application forms for the program. In 1988, grants ranged in size from $360 to $2,097 each; a total of $60,000 has been given out over the first three years of the program. The grant program is administered by a nine person Educational Technology Committee comprised of teachers, librarians, and administrators. This committee was first established in 1983 to coordinate computer activities throughout the district.

a few people may be able to teach themselves from the documentation provided and by experimentation, most people need a formal training program.

For example, imagine that a school decides to implement a computer-based student records system. The front office staff who will be responsible for entering data and printing reports will need a formal training course with hands-on practice in order to learn how to use the system properly. This can be achieved by sending key staff to an off-site training course, or by having a vendor representative or consultant give an on-site course. If the staff are left to learn the system on their own, it is very unlikely they will learn how to use the system properly or in a short amount of time. The availability of such training courses is obviously an important consideration in buying such a system.

The same need for training exists among the teaching staff, even though they may already have computer experience or computer courses in their degree programs. For example, suppose that the school is to start participating in a telecommunications project that lets students in different locations interact via electronic mail and computer conferences. Each teacher involved in the project needs to be shown how to use the telecommunications network involved if they are to assist their students. Demonstrations and hands-on training will be needed, otherwise the teachers will not be able to work with the students and the project may flop. In-service training conducted at the school is to be preferred over off-site training since this makes it easier for all teachers to participate.

The important thing to understand about computer training is that just because a person understands how to use the computer for one application, they do not automatically know how to use it for any other application. While it is true that the more a person uses a computer, the easier it becomes to learn about new applications; it is not the case that they can teach themselves or won't need training. Each time new hardware or software is introduced in a school, some sort of training is likely to be needed. Thus, computer training activities must be ongoing to accommodate new staff, equipment, and applications.

A major issue that arises in conjunction with any training activity is payment or released time. Many teachers and staff members are willing to participate in computer training activities on their own time since they feel that this training improves their professional qualifications and skills. However, other individuals feel that such training is work-related and they should be compensated in some fashion for participation. Most districts recognize the need to provide released time for training activities and funds are often provided by grants. In many cases, staff and teacher participation in computer training is credited towards salary increases or bonuses.[3]

SECURITY

Another important implementation issue is security. If adequate precautions aren't taken with hardware and software, it is not likely to stay around long enough to be put to use. Schools are notorious for theft and vandalism, and computers are not immune from this fact of life. In addition, new forms of computer abuse and crime, such as hacking and viruses, require vigilance on the part of educational administrators.

As a general rule, all computer hardware and equipment should be bolted down or locked in some fashion so that it cannot be removed. Many companies make special cases or pads that allow machines to be locked on a desk or table. This includes keyboards, disk drives, monitors, printers, and any other free-standing components. Connecting cables should be screwed in so that they can't be easily re-

---

[3] For discussion of training costs, see Beach and Lindahl (1984) or Hoover and Gould (1982).

moved. Software needs to be kept in a locked cabinet or storage area and signed in/out by students, staff, and teachers when used. Only backup copies of programs should be used; the master copy should not be distributed and kept in a separate secure place (like a locked office cabinet or school safe). In addition, labs and classrooms that contain computers or software should be physically secure in terms of bolt-type locks and barred windows. An alarm system is strongly recommended.

Some schools like to encourage teachers, staff, and students to take computers home for training or special projects. This raises problems in terms of security in the borrower's home and vehicle (as well as off-site insurance coverage). Ideally, "loaner" machines and software should be separate from regularly used equipment so that loss does not disrupt routine computer activities. Portable and lap-top computers are well suited for this purpose; they can be kept in a locked compartment (car trunk, desk drawer, briefcase) when not in use.

Special precautions against "hacking" are required for computers equipped with modems. Computer-wise students can use the modem to illegally access other computers and cause havoc. Clearly, it is not advisable to allow computers with modems to be used without supervision. Modems can be removed and kept in storage when not in use. The same advice applies to computers equipped with modems for administrative use that are open to staff.

Another security problem is the creation and spread of computer viruses. A computer virus is a self-replicating program that contaminates a hard disk and may cause damage to any software stored on that disk. Virus infection can be prevented by so-called "vaccine" or antiviral programs that are kept on the hard disk which prevent virus programs from copying themselves to the hard disk. It is strongly recommended that all machines with hard disks have such a vaccine program installed. Viruses are especially serious problems in networks since they easily infect all machines that belong to the network.

Good supervision of students and staff when using computers is the best measure to prevent vandalism and abuse. Furthermore, if all students and staff are enthusiastic about and supportive of activities, it is likely that the equipment and software will be treated with respect and care. On the other hand, if computers are limited to certain students or staff, they may be resented and become the targets of anger and frustration.

MAINTENANCE

Like any other technology, computers eventually fail and need repair. In addition, both hardware and software are subject to the need to upgrade in order to stay useful. If computer systems are not maintained properly, they tend to fall into disuse quickly.

Actual repair or replacement of computer hardware is not the real problem—diagnosing what is wrong is what takes a lot of time. Unless it is something very obvious (like the screen burns out), it is often difficult to determine the source of a problem. First, it is necessary to pinpoint whether the problem is due to hardware or software. Secondly, the exact location of the problem needs to be isolated so that the faulty component can be serviced. In many cases, the problem is intermitent and only happens at certain times. In other cases, there is really nothing wrong—a cable is loose or unplugged, or a switch setting has been accidently changed.

People who work with computers on a regular basis learn some basic troubleshooting techniques. This includes systematically testing each component or option to find out what works and what doesn't. Keeping detailed notes during this process is important. Trying the same operation on a different machine or switching components is a good way to narrow down a problem—if the same problem occurs on more than one machine, it must be caused by the switched disk or component.

Software and hardware vendors usually provide technical hotlines that can be called when problems arise. They may be able to suggest solutions or things to try to determine the problem. They will need complete details of the system, version or model numbers, and the conditions that the problem occurs under. If you have a working relationship with a local computer dealer, they may be able to provide help over the telephone or in-store service. In the case of personal computers, it is a simple matter to take the failed component (or the entire system) to a service center for examination and repair.

Software updates pose a special nuisance. All software vendors make periodic improvements to their programs that include new features. Updates are usually available at a nominal cost to existing users. Unfortunately, newer versions of programs are not always totally compatible with earlier versions. This means that a file created with an earlier version may not work exactly the same way (if at all) with newer versions. When new versions of operating systems are installed, programs that used to work with the previous version may not work. Because of these problems, many people are reluctant to upgrade software. On the other hand, if you don't upgrade you forgo the new features, and in the case of operating systems, the ability to run new programs developed for them.

The dilemma for the educational administrator is who is going to be responsible for maintenance tasks. If a school or district has a computer coordinator, maintenance duties would naturally be part of their job. However, repair of hardware still requires outside service. In some districts and larger schools, there may be a computer technician who is responsible for repairing computer hardware. Another possibility is to have a service contract with a local computer store or company who takes care of all maintenance responsibilities for both hardware and software. What is not a satisfactory alternative is to expect teachers and staff to maintain equipment.

SUMMARY

In this chapter we talked about some of the major factors that play a role in the successful implementation of computers, including facilities, staffing, training, security, and maintenance. Although we discussed each of these factors separately, they are closely dependent. For example, the creation of a computer lab is going to necessitate someone to supervise and run the lab; the availability of a computer coordinator necessitates someone to organize training activities; proper training may reduce maintenance problems.

Each one of these implementation factors needs careful and ongoing attention from administrators. The best way to deal with all of these issues is by addressing them explicitly in computer planning activities (see Chapter 7). Most things boil down to being included in the budget. If they are known about and put into the budget, there is a good chance they will be taken care of (budget cuts aside). Even unexpected events, such as new products, new application ideas, or projects that don't work out, can be accommodated in a general way by an experienced administrator.

EXERCISES

1. Imagine that you have been given an unlimited grant for as many computers as you want. How would you locate them in a school? Indicate the applications they would be used for.
2. Interview a school computer coordinator to find out what they do. Based upon this interview, make up a description of a "day in the life" of a computer coordinator. Document it with slides/video if possible.
3. Prepare a teacher and staff training schedule for the upcoming school term. You decide what applications will be involved.
4. Develop a security plan for your school or district. List the costs associated with each measure. Check out insurance coverage for computers—does it cost extra?
5. After talking to pertinent school personnel, make up a list of typical computer problems and how they are resolved. What problems are not handled very well. How could this be improved?

CHECKLIST FOR COMPUTER IMPLEMENTATION

Facilities

☐ Should computers for administration be located in individual offices or shared areas?

☐ Should computers for instruction be located in classrooms or labs/libraries?

☐ Are proper furnishings, storage areas, power outlets, and air conditioning available?

Staffing

☐ Is a computer coordinator available?

☐ Are computer assistants or aides available?

☐ What kind of consultants will be needed?

Training

☐ What kind of formal training will be planned for office and teaching staff?

☐ How will ongoing training be conducted?

☐ How will staff be compensated for training participation?

Security

☐ Is all computer equipment secure?

☐ Is all software kept in locked storage areas?

☐ Are doors and windows in rooms containing computers secure?

☐ Are special precautions taken for mobile or take-home equipment?

☐ Is all use of modems carefully supervised?

☐ Are all machines with hard disks protected against virus infection?

Maintenance

☐ Have provisions been made for diagnosing computer problems?

☐ Is maintenance responsibility for computers clearly defined?

☐ Is responsibility for software upgrading clearly defined?

7

Planning for Computers

One of the essential elements of good administration is planning. Administering computers is no different. Plans for all aspects of computer use are needed: to determine what kind of hardware and software are needed, to make sure that implementation goes smoothly, and to ensure that proper budgets are submitted. Such plans result in policies that guide decisions and procedures to be followed in daily management.

It is critical to understand that computer use in schools is a major administrative concern at all levels. Once computers are introduced for either office or classroom applications, they tend to impact all aspects of school functions. They will significantly affect the activities of staff, teachers, and students regardless of how they are used. They will also affect facilities, scheduling, budgets, and politics. Because of their pervasive effects, it is essential that computer use in schools be guided by explicit and well thought-out plans, rather than impromptu or seat-of-the-pants decisions.

This chapter discusses some of the issues that should be addressed by computer utilization plans. Not all issues will be equally important to all levels of administration; however, every administrator should at least give consideration to whether an issue applies to their school situation.[1]

---

[1] For more extensive discussion of planning computer use in schools, see Bank and Williams (1987) or Pogrow (1983).

IDENTIFYING GOALS AND OBJECTIVES

The first issue is probably the most important since it defines almost all other aspects of planning for computers in a school or district. The issue is the purpose or goals of using computers in a particular school or school system. There are many possible goals, such as:

- to better prepare students for jobs or college
- to improve the efficiency of administrative operations
- to deliver better quality education to all students
- to achieve more accurate budgets and controls of funds
- to give students and teachers more classroom options.

Such goals tend to be relatively general statements of intent which must be translated into specific objectives that can be accomplished, such as these examples:

- increase reading and writing skills in primary grades
- reduce the costs/time required for attendance tracking
- get more minority students to take science and math
- send out more detailed progress reports to parents
- provide better vocational counseling to graduates.

When specific objectives have been defined, it then becomes clear what kind of computing activities are desired and appropriate.

Setting goals and developing objectives for computer use requires the input and concensus of every group that will be affected by their use including: staff, teachers, students, parents, and board members. There are likely to be many differences of opinion about the goals of computing, and each opinion should be weighed. The best technique is to simply list all the ideas, and then have each group make its recommendations followed by a final selection based upon other considerations, such as state or district mandates or priorities. Objectives should be developed for the goals selected, and these objectives presented for ratification to the initial groups.

The importance of establishing goals and objectives in this fashion cannot be overemphasized. If the different stake holders do not participate in the decision process, they are not likely to be very supportive of computer activities and may even oppose it. Furthermore, the goal definition process provides an opportunity to present different ideas about computer use to the school community and can serve as an orientation. Instead of one person (e.g., yourself) trying to convince everyone of the potential of computers, computer literate staff, teachers, and parents can accomplish the task more effectively. These individuals may form the nucleus of a computer advisory group that meets regularly to provide advice and consultation for computer-related decisions on an ex-officio or ad-hoc basis.

Without explicit goals and objectives, computer use is likely to develop in a haphazard manner based upon the interest of certain staff members or teachers. Such haphazard development is not likely to address the highest priority use of computers or result in the most effective solutions. For example, a computer science teacher may obtain some very powerful computers through a grant to be used for an advanced placement programming class. In the meantime, the majority of students are failing basic literacy criteria. While the programming application may well be very worthwhile, it probably does not represent the best use of computer resources in the school, and is likely to lead to resentment on the part of many teachers, students, and parents.

Establishing goals and achieving concensus are not easy tasks. However, they are far easier tasks than trying to defend and successfully implement computer applications that do not have the full support of the school community. In addition, they make many other computer-related decisions, such as what hardware/software to obtain and where to locate the computers, much easier to make.

ACQUIRING HARDWARE/SOFTWARE

The capabilities of the hardware and software selected for school use play a major role in determining what types of applications are possible. Some examples are obvious. If one of the applications desired in desktop publishing, it will be necessary to acquire appropriate software (i.e., page composition programs) and hardware (e.g., laser printers). Other examples of this principle are more subtle. Consider an objective to improve the communication skills of primary grade students. While language arts drills may help, a word processing program specifically designed for young children is likely to be more on target.

Educational administrators cannot be expected to be familiar with the particular capabilities or features of all the different hardware and software available. They should, however, expect staff members, teachers, consultants, and vendors involved in selection decisions to identify how specific hardware and software meets defined objectives. There are many ways this information can be obtained:

- on-site demonstrations or previews
- presentations/discussions at conferences
- published reviews or evaluation studies
- recommendations from educators who have used the equipment or programs
- certifications or endorsements by professional organizations or state agencies.

Administrators should be wary of selecting hardware or software because of its reputation rather than because it meets a defined need. Even the most well-respected computer or program will not help if it is a square peg in a round hole. If you are looking for a simple attendance program, there is no need to buy a sophisticated student management system, unless your objective is to relate attendance to all other aspects of student data.

In most cases, computer equipment and software will be purchased through a bid process. In the case of complete systems, your school or district will issue a request for bids which states the functionality desired and any constraints on cost, operation, or delivery time. This bid request will be sent to interested vendors who then submit proposals. The bid is awarded to the vendor who is judged to best meet the requirements specified. This bidding process works equally well for situations where the specific hardware or software is unknown as well as when it is known. In the former situation, the vendor is expected to provide their solution to the needs; in the latter, the focus is on the provision of the required equipment or programs in the most expedient manner.

When purchasing any hardware or software for schools, the most important criteria should be the nature of the training and support to be provided by the vendor. Time to learn how to use computers and software is always in short supply at any school. The more help the vendor can provide, the smoother things will go. Since there will be staff and teacher turnover, as well as new applications, it is critical that the training and support be provided on a long-term and ongoing basis.

An important thing to keep in mind about computers is that they tend to become "obsolete" within 3–5 years of their acquisition. The pace of development in the computer field is such that newer hardware and software have considerably more capability than systems only a few years old. Thus, it is to be anticipated that hardware and software will probably be replaced every 3–5 years, even though there is nothing really wrong with it. Older systems can usually be donated to community groups (or possibly other schools) that do not have any computer equipment.

IMPLEMENTATION SCHEDULING

One of the major planning duties of an administrator is to schedule things so that chaos is avoided. If you review the various components to successful computer implementation, as discussed in Chapter 6, you will realize that a lot of scheduling is needed. A timeline chart is needed that takes into account the interaction among planning, selection, facilities, staffing, training, and maintenance tasks. Figure 7.1 illustrates the basic dimensions of such a chart.

Here are some of the tasks that might appear on this chart:

- Create a computer advisory committee.
- Develop a school/district computer plan specifying goals and objectives.
- Present a plan to the school board for review/approval.
- Evaluate suitable hardware and software.
- Conduct pilot study.
- Identify facilities required.
- Identify staff required.
- Identify training needed.
- Estimate costs and develop budgets.
- Submit funding requests.
- Issue bids/select hardware and software.
- Award bids/order hardware and software.
- Make facility changes.
- Hire computer staff needed.
- Install hardware and software.

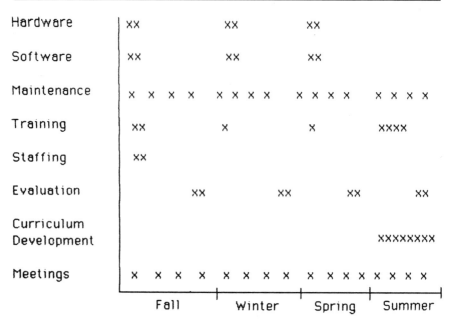

Figure 7.1. Illustration of a planning chart showing number of weeks allocated to different computer activities over the school year.

- Conduct initial training.
- Field test hardware/software.
- Conduct preliminary evaluation.
- Present results of preliminary evaluation.
- Conduct addditional training.
- Full implementation of system.
- Conduct periodic maintenance.
- Evaluate first term/year results.
- Report first term/year results.
- Identify new hardware/software needed.
- Identify new facilities/staff/training needed.
- Review/revise computer plan.

Many of these steps would need to be broken down into substeps. For example, "making facility changes" could involve building modifications, new furniture, electrical work, and installing alarms or new locks. "Hiring computer staff needed" may involve advertising positions, interviewing candidates, and completing all paperwork. A great many tasks will involve meetings that must be scheduled, prepared for, conducted, and the results disseminated or followed up on.

Preparing a schedule for computer implementation is also the best way to help identify the staff needed for computer activities. For each task, the type of skills and the amount of time required can be estimated. In the process of making these estimates, it will become clear what kind of staff will be needed and how much each person will be involved in the project.

Incidently, there are many project management programs available that can streamline the scheduling process. Such programs automatically produce charts showing all tasks that need to be completed. If scheduling is a major aspect of your job, you will undoubtedly want to use one of these programs. Administrators who are responsible for implementing large-scale projects (such as the building of new schools or district-wide evaluation studies) will probably want to investigate PERT (Program Evaluation and Review Technique) or CPM (Critical Path Method) software.[2] On the other hand, for routine scheduling activities, spreadsheets will likely fill the need.

One important aspect of scheduling is to identify reoccurring events. A lot of tasks must be repeated on a regular basis. For example, computer plans must be reviewed and revised each year, training needs to be repeated for new hires, and additional hardware and software will be required. There is a tendency to carry out such tasks the first time and then to forget about them. Including them in the schedule reminds everyone that the tasks should reoccur.

One important lesson about planning implementation of any technology is to go slowly and anticipate lots of setbacks and obstacles. Any use of computers in a school is a major innovation that involves new ways of doing things. It takes time for people to become comfortable with new approaches and to learn how to take advantage of them. For this reason, the best strategy to follow in any computer project is to always begin with a small pilot project, no matter how good the idea is or how enthusiastic the project team is. The pilot project will identify potential problems that need to be solved before the full-scale project is implemented.

Figure 7.2 summarizes some of the major steps that need to be taken into account when planning an implementation schedule.

---

[2] For more about PERT applications in education, see Case (1969) or Hai (1977).

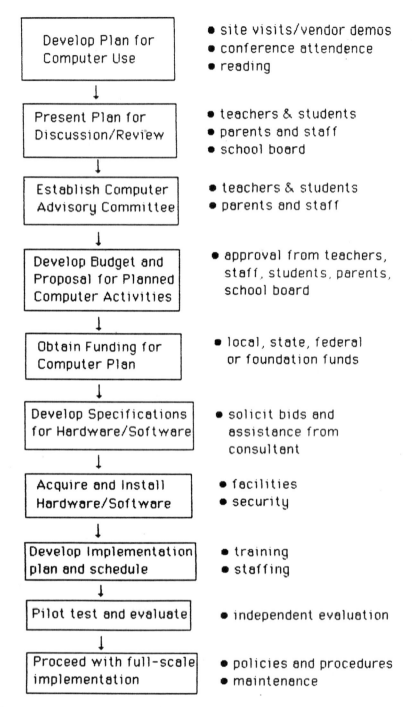

Develop Plan for Computer Use	• site visits/vendor demos • conference attendance • reading
Present Plan for Discussion/Review	• teachers & students • parents and staff • school board
Establish Computer Advisory Committee	• teachers & students • parents and staff
Develop Budget and Proposal for Planned Computer Activities	• approval from teachers, staff, students, parents, school board
Obtain Funding for Computer Plan	• local, state, federal or foundation funds
Develop Specifications for Hardware/Software	• solicit bids and assistance from consultant
Acquire and Install Hardware/Software	• facilities • security
Develop Implementation plan and schedule	• training • staffing
Pilot test and evaluate	• independent evaluation
Proceed with full-scale implementation	• policies and procedures • maintenance

Figure 7.2.   Major steps in planning computer activities.

EVALUATION

Educational administrators are accountable for what happens (or doesn't happen) in a school system. When applied to the computer domain, this means a responsibility to evaluate the effectiveness of computer uses. Evaluation data are needed to determine whether specific applications are achieving the intended results.

The first consideration in designing an evaluation study is to determine what should be measured. In the case of administrative applicaations, this could include:

- time to complete tasks
- amount of work completed
- quality of results
- number of errors
- employee satisfaction.

For instructional applications, dimensions that could be measured include:

- achievement scores
- grades
- attendance
- graduation
- disciplinary actions
- student esteem
- teacher/parent satisfaction.

The appropriate thing to measure will depend upon the specific objectives of computer use. For example, if the objective was to reduce the costs of processing student records, then measuring the time taken to process student records before and after computerization would be a way to determine if costs were reduced. Similarly, if the objective was to improve student involvement, measures of attendance, graduation and satisfaction would be relevant.

There are a number of different ways to collect the data desired. In the case of job performance measures, records can be kept of the number of transactions performed, the time taken to complete transactions, or the quality of the results. To measure attitudes, questionnaires or surveys are usually used. Most academic measures (e.g., grades, test scores, attendance, or disciplinary actions) can be taken from student records. Qualitative data are important as well. Written journals kept by students or teachers help capture many details not depicted in quantitative data. Similarly, photographs and videotapes help document changes and events that cannot be portrayed by numbers.

Computer utilization data are important as well. It is useful to know how often computers were used, for what purposes, and by whom. An increased pattern of computer use is often one of the best indications of the success of a project—after all, people don't continue to use something unless they find it worthwhile. Furthermore, computer usage data should be easy to obtain since it can be collected automatically by the computer whenever people sign-on to use it.

School environments provide many evaluation opportunities that are not available in other settings. For example, they are ideal for conducting longitudinal studies of computer effects over time. It is possible to follow the same students or staff over a number of years and measure that long-term impact of computer use on their achievement or work performance. Another advantage of school settings is that there are often naturally occuring control groups consisting of students/classes taught by the same teachers who do not participate in computer activities for some reason. Finally, since students and teachers are always part of a larger group, it is possible to compare the effects on specific individuals with the overall effects on the group.

There are three important lessons to be learned about conducting evaluations. The first is that they must be planned early in a project so that baseline data can be collected before computers are introduced. Secondly, the objectives of computer use must be clear-cut, otherwise it will be difficult to know what to measure. Data should be collected to answer a specific question about whether a certain computer application works or doesn't work. If the question has not been articulated clearly, there is little chance that an evaluation will produce data that answers the question. Thirdly, evaluation studies should be conducted by independent parties not directly involved in the application (preferable not even affiliated with the school or district). This leads to more objectivity and less political influence on the results and conclusions.

ESTABLISHING POLICIES AND PROCEDURES

To ensure that computer implementation goes smoothly, it is highly desirable to have as many potential problem areas as possible addressed by explicit policy statements and procedures. The process for formulating such policies and procedures ensures that some consideration is given to the causes, consequences, and responses associated with each issue.

Piracy (illegal copying) of software and privacy of student record databases are two areas that require clear policy statements and appropriate procedures since both are subject to legal actions. A written warning about illegal copying should be read by all staff and teachers and posted in all areas where computers are used. The computer coordinator or the person responsible for supervising software use should ensure that proper site licenses or multiple copies are available for all programs. Privacy rights can be ensured by only allowing authorized staff access to databases through the use of passwords. Those staff members who have access need to be aware of who they can provide information and reports to.

Policies will probably be needed when scheduling computer use. A reservation or sign-out system will be necessary for labs and mobile computers. Rules about unsupervised use and take-home use (if allowed) will be required. Provisions for teacher preview of software and extracurricular use by students will also be needed. If computer resources are limited, scheduling policies become particularly critical.

Procedures will be needed to ensure that backups of programs and data are made routinely. Backups are especially important for all financial and student records since loss of this data could be catastrophic. Many offices back up their data at least once a week and keep the backup disks in a safe or off-site location (e.g., district office or local bank). In the classroom, teachers should teach students about backing up their data as well. Losing files that contain class assignments is something that students and teachers will want to avoid.

Criteria will need to be established for staff and teacher computer competencies used in hiring and training activities. In many states, computer competencies will be included in credential requirements; however, additional competencies may be needed for specific school applications. Staff competencies will cover the use of basic applications software (e.g., word processing, spreadsheets, databases, telecommunications) as well as specific administrative programs for attendance, registration, and grading. Procedures will be needed for training new staff on the specific programs used in the school.

Policies for encouraging teacher and staff involvement with computers are needed. Learning how to use computers and putting them to use in classrooms or school operations typically take an enormous amount of effort. Incentives of some kind are important in motivating individuals to start with and continue using computers. Since these incentives are likely to involve salary increases, released time, professional development grants, or career advancements, they need to be included in budgets and personnel plans.

Finally, policies will be needed to ensure equal access to computers in the classroom for all minority students. It is quite common for computer activities to be dominated by the more academically advanced students in a school, while "at risk" students get little time on the computer. A more subtle inequity is when minority students are restricted to remedial activities, such as drills or games, while better-off students get more challenging applications. One area requiring special attention is in encouraging female students to use the computer; studies show that without specific intervention, computer activities will become male-dominated.[3] There is absolutely no reason to believe that academic ability or sex is a determining factor in a student's success using the computer. All students should have equal opportunity in terms of computer use.

As this discussion of policies and procedures illustrates, planning for computers can impact many aspects of school operations. This fact underscores the pervasiveness of computers and why it is so important to adequately prepare for them.

SUMMARY

This chapter discussed some of the factors that need to be taken into account when planning for computer use in schools. The significance of developing goals and objectives for computer use was emphasized. Clearly defined objectives make it easier to determine

---

[3] For a discussion, see Collis (1988).

what kind of computer applications are appropriate for a given school, as well as what kind of hardware and software are needed. When acquiring computer equipment, certain procedures should be followed, such as bid specifications and adequate evaluation. To ensure smooth implementation, scheduling of all tasks associated with computer use should be done as a planning activity. Planning activities should also include evaluation measures for all computer uses. Explicit policies and procedures will be needed for many aspects of computer uses, including piracy and privacy precautions, back-ups, scheduling, competencies, training, and equal access.

Almost all of the planning aspects outlined in this chapter have financial or budget implications. In the next chapter, we will address the cost factors associated with computer use.

EXERCISES

1. Develop a set of goals and objectives for computer use in a school or district. Consult as many different members of the school community as possible in their formulation.
2. Create a bid request for hardware and/or software for a specific school or district.
3. Make up a master schedule for one week of computer use in a school.
4. Write up an evaluation plan for computing activity in a school or district.
5. Write up a set of policies for administrative and classroom use of computers in a school or district.

CHECKLIST FOR COMPUTER PLANNING

Goals & Objectives

☐ Does a statement of goals and objectives for computer use exist?
☐ Have goals and objectives for computer use been formulated and reviewed by all members of school community?

(continued)

Acquiring Hardware/Software

☐ Are goals/objectives reflected in the choice of hardware and software?

☐ Does a procurement procedure exist for buying hardware and software?

☐ Does the procurement process place proper emphasis on vendor support?

Implementation Scheduling

☐ Does a timeline chart exist that encompasses all planning tasks?

☐ Are all reoccuring tasks included on the chart?

☐ Are all meetings shown on the chart?

Evaluation

☐ Have the dimensions to be measured been clearly identified?

☐ Have the data collection methods been identified?

☐ Will computer utilization data be collected?

☐ Will evaluation activities be conducted by a neutral party?

Establishing Policies & Procedures

☐ Do policies for software piracy and privacy of databases exist?

☐ Does a policy exist for the scheduling of computer resources?

☐ Do procedures exist for backup of data?

☐ Have the computer competencies required of staff been explicitly defined?

☐ Do incentives and compensation exist for computer activities?

☐ Are there procedures that ensure equal access to computers for all school students?

8

Financing Computers

This chapter discusses the financial aspects of computers in education, including cost/benefits analysis, budgets, funding sources, and expenses. Cost/benefits analysis plays an important role in making good decisions about worthwhile computer uses. To the extent that the successful implementation of computers depends upon having adequate resources available, knowing how to budget and secure proper funding for computers are critical tasks for an administrator. Finally, computer expenses need to be managed wisely like any other category of school costs.

COST/BENEFITS

A good place to begin a discussion of the financial aspects of computers is with the topic of cost/benefits analysis. Cost/benefits analysis involves comparing the expected outcomes of using computers against the costs involved and deciding whether it is worthwhile. Not all applications of computers are cost-effective, and any consideration of their use should begin with a cost/benefits analysis. As such, cost/benefits analysis is an important component of any study in determining the feasibility of computer activities in a school system.

There are many different types of cost/benefits analysis.[1] A fundamental distinction to be made is whether the purpose of the analysis

---

[1] For more information about cost/benefits analysis, see Kearsley (1982) or Wagner (1982).

is to evaluate cost-savings (improved efficiency), increased effectiveness (better results for the same costs), or improvement in productivity (doing more work with fewer resources). This distinction is important because different kinds of models and data are involved.

The simplest kind of cost/benefits analysis is the resource requirements model in which different cost components are compared between two approaches with an assumption of equal effectiveness. The purpose of the model is to determine which approach is less costly. For example, suppose that you wanted to compare manual versus computerized grade reporting. You would add up all costs for the two approaches (e.g., labor, materials, equipment) for a given time period and see which has lower total costs. This kind of analysis is easy to do with a calculator or spreadsheet (see Figure 8.1).

Suppose, however, that what you are really interested in measuring is increased productivity. In other words, you want to know if attendance can be tracked better for less money. The resource requirements model can't help you with this question because it makes the assumption of equal effectiveness. Instead, you must use a productivity model, such as a return on investment (ROI) model. In an ROI model, you examine the ratio of the output (in this case, completed grade reports) to some resource measure (e.g., the length of time taken to complete the reports). The larger the ratio, the better the return on investment. For example, if it takes 40 hours to produce the reports for 1,000 students using manual methods (ROI = 25), but 20 hours to do the reports for 2,000 students (ROI = 100) using the computer, the automated system has improved productivity by a factor of four.

One cost/benefits measure that is often used in school settings is the cost per student. To calculate this measure, you simply add up all the costs associated with a certain approach, and then divide this total by the total number of students served. For example, if you were trying to evaluate the worth of a computer-based quidance system, you could calculate the cost per student of providing counseling via teachers versus using the computer. In order to do this calculation, you would need to know the average duration of the counseling sessions at present and when using the computer.

This last example raises one of the most important things to understand about conducting any type of cost/benefits analysis—the validity of the analysis depends almost completely upon the quality of the data used (remember GIGO—Garbage In, Garbage Out). A

COST OF COMPARISON OF COMPUTER VS MANUAL GRADING
Number of Students = 1000

COMPONENT		MANUAL	COMPUTER
Labor:			
	Time to type report	$1,500	
	Time to enter grades		$250
Equipment:			
	Typewriter	$600	
	Computer & Software		$1,500
	Scanner		$500
Materials:			
	Report Cards	$250	
	Printer Paper		$10
	OCR Score Forms		$150
Training:			
	Learn to type cards	$12	
	Learn to use program		$48
	Learn to use scanner		$18
	TOTALS	$3,362	$2,476
	COST SAVINGS		$886

Note: This spreadsheet lets you compare the costs of computer-based versus manual grade reports for different numbers of students (entered in C2). Labor and materials costs depend upon the number of students entered. (Break-even point for this example is 621 students.)

Figure 8.1. Cost comparison using a spreadsheet.

lot of effort may be required to collect and check the data needed for a cost/benefits study. However, the effort is usually well worth the trouble because it leads to decisions that are based on facts instead of fancy.

A cost/benefits analysis should be conducted prior to any major funding request for computer projects. First of all, it will define the payoffs of the project and provide a basis for the request. Secondly, it should identify the cost components involved in the project and result in a more complete budget estimate. Thirdly, it will establish evaluation criteria that can be used later to decide if the project worked or not, and if it is worth further support.

BUDGETING

Preparing budgets is probably the single most important task of an administrator. Budgets represent the action plan distilled from many discussions and meetings. They specify what resources will be available in terms of equipment, staff, facilities, and materials. Budgets for computer activities reflect how computers will be used in a school or district, and hence, determine their potential impact on students and staff.

Preparing a budget for computing activities is no different than preparing a budget for any other school activity. There will be some initial start-up costs and some reoccurring items. The trick is to be sure that all costs are taken into account so that a project doesn't fall short of money. It is the completeness of the budget, rather than the estimates for individual items, that usually causes problems.

Figure 8.2 lists a sample annual budget for school computing activities. Note that the hardware and software costs are capital costs and could be amortized over the expected lifetime of the systems (three years) if they are leased. One of the difficulties of budgeting computer activities is that the cost items are often spread out in many different places when traditional budget categories are used. For this reason, it is a good idea to prepare the computer budget as a whole, and then transfer the items to the appropriate categories of the master budget.

Spreadsheets are highly valuable for budget activities. Not only does the spreadsheet make it easy to accurately calculate all totals, but it also makes it easy to change numbers as the budget is being reviewed and finalized. The effets of cuts or reductions can be calculated immediately. Furthermore, once a template has been created for a certain budget category, it can be reused again, saving a lot of time.

200	SALARIES		
	Asst. Principal (¼ rel. time)	$10,000	
	Admin. Asst. (½ time)	$ 9,500	
	Computer Coordinator	$31,000	
	Lab Asst.	$18,000	
	Teachers (10 × ¼ rel. time)	$17,000	
	Librarian (⅓ rel. time)	$ 9,000	
	Consultants (10 days @ $500/day)	$ 5,000	
			$99,500
230	COMPUTER SOFTWARE		
	Administrative programs	$ 2,500	
	Instructional programs	$ 3,000	
	Desktop Publishing software	$ 1,000	
			$ 6,500
240	COMPUTER SUPPLIES		
	Paper	$ 500	
	Disks	$ 150	
	Ribbons & Toner	$ 450	
	Periodicals/Books	$ 300	
			$ 1,400
250	COMPUTER-RELATED TRAVEL		
	Conference Participations	$ 2,000	
	Site Visits	$ 1,000	
			$ 3,000
600	COMPUTER FACILITIES		
	Furniture	$ 2,000	
	Building Modifications	$ 1,500	
	Security Equipment	$ 1,500	
	Air Conditioning (computer lab)	$ 1,500	
	Phone Lines	$ 600	
			$ 6,600
700	COMPUTER EQUIPMENT		
	Personal computers (32 @ $1,500)	$48,000	
	Dot matrix printers (8 @ $300)	$ 2,400	
	Laser printers (2 @ $3,000)	$ 6,000	
	Network interfaces (12 @ $500)	$ 6,000	
	Modems (6 @ $250)	$ 1,500	
	Annual Maintenance contract	$ 1,500	
			$65,400
			$182,400

Figure 8.2. Sample annual computer budget.

FUNDING SOURCES

Obtaining funds for computer activities has been a major problem for all educational administrators. No educational system has an abundance of money, and there are always many worthwhile projects competing for the limited funds that are available. Let's look at the possible sources of funding for computer activities.

The regular school budget (from local and state appropriations) is a good source for ongoing cost items, such as supplies, inservice training, phone lines, maintenance, and professional development activities. These items are not substantial and should come out of an operating budget like any other school activity. To the extent that computers play an important role in classroom or administrative functions, they can be justified as regular expenditures.

Acquiring the initial hardware or software needed for a project is another matter. This money is typically obtained via grants from federal programs or foundations. Most of the large computer companies, such as Apple, Digital Equipment Corp., and IBM, have grant programs that donate hardware and software. The U.S. Department of Education and the National Science Foundation have provided many grants over the years for research in the educational computing area. For example, Figure 8.3 lists some of the funding categories in the Department of Education budget that could be used to fund technology.

Local sources of funding should not be overlooked. Some schools have posted special bond issues to acquire computer equipment and facilities. Local companies or agencies may be willing to donate money (to help raise it) if they are convinced of the importance of computers for improved schooling. In some cases, the donations may be used to support computer activities that directly impact their activities, such as providing potential or present employees with computer skills needed in their operations. Examples include word processing and desktop publishing, database management, financial and accounting software, and computer-aided design (CAD).

Getting the initial funds needed for computing activities is usually the most difficult part of the funding process. It is most certainly going to require the writing of proposals and showing of many presentations to potential funding agencies. Figure 8.4 lists some of the most important components to be included in a proposal or presenta-

Program	1989 Appropriation
Education Consolidation & Improvement Act	
Chapter 1 Block Grants	4,060.2
Chapter 2 Block Grants	540.5
National Diffusion Network	10.2
Elementary & Secondary Education Act	
Title VII—Bilingual Education	13.1
Education for Economic Security Act	
Title II—Math & Science State Grants	108.9
Title VII—Magnet Schools	115.0
Higher Education Act	
Title V-C—Leadership in Educ Admin	4.4
Title V-D—McAuliffe Fellowships	1.9
Fund Improvement in Post-Sec Educ (FIPSE)	13.6
Education for the Handicapped Act	
State Grants	1,747.7
Technology for Special Educ	4.8
Early Childhood Educ	23.4
Media and Captioning	13.2
Personnel Development	66.4
Vocational Education Act	
Title II—State Grants	835.2
High Technology Demonstrations	6.0
Adult Education Act	
State Grants	148.2

Figure 8.3.   U.S. Department of Education Funding programs.

tion. In addition to a good proposal, the support of teachers, parents, students, staff, board members, community leaders, politicians, and other school administrators is going to be critical to in getting the funds needed. You should take the advantage of the information and data available from the many organizations that promote and encourage the use of computers in education (see Appendix).

Title Page
Executive Summary
Table of Contents
School Background
Rational for Computer Use
Anticipated Benefits
Implementation Plan
Staff Involved/Required
Computer Hardware/Software
Budget
Summary
Appendices

Figure 8.4.   Critical elements of a good proposal.

EXPENSES

Once you have successfully raised the money for computer facilities and put your plan into operation, the final step is to properly manage costs. There are many ways that computer expenses can be contained. For example, buying computer supplies, such as paper and disks in bulk and "generic" form, can cut these costs dramatically. However, the most significant cost item is usually training, or lack of it. The training problem starts with the selection of the hardware and software (mostly the latter). If a machine or program is difficult to use, a lot of time will be wasted by staff trying to figure out how to use it. On the other hand, if training is needed, failure to provide it in a timely fashion will have the same effect—poor or nonuse of computers. Buying hardware and software that is easy to use minimizes training problems, and hence, loss of productivity.

Another common way of wasting money with computers is to buy hardware and software that is not really needed or that doesn't meet the real needs. Some computer vendors are notorious for convincing culpable school board members or administrators to buy their latest new toys. In other cases, decisions are made to buy certain hardware or software that does not match what was requested because of price or supplier considerations. Saving a few dollars on something that will never get used is false economy. The answer to this problem is to make sure that the ultimate users specify or approve what is to be purchased.

Although computers are relatively reliable, the costs of maintaining a school full of machines can be significant. The usual rule of thumb for maintenance costs is about five percent of the purchase price per year. Thus, if you have $50,000 worth of computer equipment, you can estimate your annual maintenance costs to be $2,500. Components with moving parts, such as keyboards, disk drives, and printers, are likely to need servicing the most. As with most equipment, a good preventive maintenance program can reduce the amount of repair and replacement needed. It is well worth having things checked and cleaned on a regular basis by a competent technician. Some larger schools with a lot of computers send someone from the plant staff to the service technician courses offered by computer vendors to provide in-house maintenance capability.

One of the things that most administrators are not prepared for when they get involved with computers is "computeritus." As staff members and teachers start to use computers, they typically discover many new programs and hardware capabilities that they must have. For every need they satisfy, computers seem to create five new ones. Thus, administrators should be wary of an exploding demand for more computers and software that can be created once they have been introduced. This is when cost/benefits analysis and goals/objectives for computer use become very important.

SUMMARY

This chapter discussed the financial aspects associated with computer use, including cost/benefits analysis, budgets, funding, and expenses. It was emphasized that conducting a cost/benefits study is essential to making sound decisions about computer use and often provides a good basis for budget and funding requests. The most important aspect of budgeting for computer activities is to ensure that all items are included. This is facilitated by making up a separate budget for computing that is then integrated into the master budget. The funding source for ongoing computer expenses should be the regular school budget; initial funding for computer projects will probably need to come from special grants. The most important computer expense item is training; not enough or too much reflects problems.

Computer activities are not inexpensive. Indeed, compared to the price of traditional school equipment, materials, and supplies, the costs may seem exorbitant. The fact is schools have historically been undercapitalized and undeveloped as far as the use of technology is concerned. Compared to other domains of human endeavor, such as agriculture, manufacturing, transportation, or warfare, we have not made any significant use of technology to improve productivity in education. The time has come to change this situation, and it requires that we spend much more on school activities than in the past. Computers represent the vanguard of this change.

EXERCISES

1. Conduct a cost/benefits analysis for a new or existing computer project. Based upon your analysis, is the project worthwhile?
2. Prepare a budget for the current or planned computer activities in a school or district. How will capital acquisitions be handled? Are new budget categories needed in the master budget to accommodate computer expenses?
3. Develop a presentation for a computer proposal. Your presentation should cover goals, rationale, implementation plan, budget summary, and funding request.
4. Make up a list of possible funding sources for computer projects that includes government programs, companies, private foundations, and local groups.
5. Examine the computer budget for an existing school or district. What expenses could be reduced? Are they spending too much or too little on training activities?
6. Collect data that show the productivity gains achieved through the use of technology in other domains over the past century. Compare this to productivity gains in education during this time. Speculate on the kinds of productivity gains that might be achieved in education through the use of technology in the next century.

CHECKLIST FOR FINANCING COMPUTERS

Cost/Benefits Analysis

☐ What type of analysis is most appropriate? (cost reduction, increased productivity)
☐ What cost data will be needed?
☐ What outcome measures will be used?

Budgeting

☐ Have the start-up capital costs been separated from the ongoing costs?
☐ Are all cost items associated with computers included?

Funding Sources

☐ Have all reoccuring cost items been covered by the regular budget?
☐ What federal/private grant programs appear to be appropriate funding sources?
☐ Have local sources of funding been investigated?

Computer Expenses

☐ Is too much or too little being spent on training staff to use computers?
☐ Are all hardware and software purchases initiated by the ultimate user?
☐ Is too much or too little being spent on maintenance of computers?

9

New Directions

This chapter discusses new directions in technology and their likely impact on education. This is important because administrators need to make plans that take such changes into account. Of course, nobody knows with certainty the exact effects of new developments, but wise administrators make decisions as more information becomes available. The developments discussed in this chapter merit watching closely.[1]

NETWORKING

The development that will most likely impact most schools in the near future is computer networking. This includes both local and telecommunications networks. Both types are likely to have similar effects in terms of increasing the popularity of electronic mail, bulletin boards, conferencing, and online databases.

Local area networks (LANs) involve linking computers together in a building or on a campus using some form of cable connection. Unlike telecommunications networks, there is no use of phone lines in a local network. Each computer that is connected to the network has a special interface circuit board that allows it to send and receive

---

[1] For discussions about the future directions of educational technology, see Perelman (1987) or the report, "Power On!," from the U.S. Congress, Office of Technology Assessment (1988).

files via the network. One computer is designated the file server and it performs all tasks associated with routing information and storing common files. The big advantage of a local network (other than files can be transferred) is that expensive peripherals, such as laser printers or CD-ROM players, can be shared by all machines on the network. Local networks can be built around existing personal computers or bought as part of an integrated learning system (discussed in Chapter 6).

Telecommunications networks involve the use of modems and telephone lines to connect one computer to another. Usually the computer being connected to (called the "host") is quite large and has an enormous amount of disk storage space. Even though the host computer may be located on the other side of the country, only a local phone call is needed to connect to it. This is accomplished by use of data transmission services that have telephone "nodes" in all major cities. There are many networks designed for school use (see the Appendix).

One of the most popular forms of networking is bulletin board systems. These systems can be operated on either a local network or a telecommunications network using a personal computer as the host. A school or district can have its own bulletin board system to provide electronic mail and conferencing capabilities to students and staff for a minimum cost. All that is required is a personal computer equipped with a modem, the bulletin board system software, and at least one dedicated phone line. However, there are a number of supervisory tasks associated with operating a bulletin board and somebody must be assigned the job of "sysop" (system operator).

The impact of networking on a school can be significant. It opens new avenues of communication for students, teachers, and staff. Electronic mail can be used in many classes by students for projects. It can also be used by staff to ensure broader and more timely involvement in school decision making. Furthermore, it can play a key role in distance learning and community outreach (see below).

Local area networks can also simplify computer use in a school and improve its cost effectiveness. Sharing of instructional software over a LAN means that computer materials are available to more students and teachers. Having software reside on a hard disk reduces the handling and security issues associated with floppy disks. More importantly, the capability to access databases and

NETWORKING IN QUEEN ANNE COUNTY*

The experience of a single school, Queen Anne County High School in Maryland, illustrates how educational networks can have a big impact on all areas of school operation. At the beginning of the 1985 school year, 32 PCjr computers were set up as a network at the school as part of the Maryland Educational Technology Network project, a joint venture with IBM who donated the equipment. The initial network connected machines located in the school library, two storage rooms adjacent to classrooms, and the special education classroom.

The network was an unqualified success right from the beginning, despite the inevitable shortage of software. However, the network allowed the available software to be accessed by all machines, and it eliminated the problems associated with handling floppy disks. Library use by students increased dramatically. To meet the demand, a compact disc with an electronic encyclopedia and an online information service, Einstein, were added to the library computer resources. A grant permitted the purchase of a college and careers database that could be accessed from any PC in the network.

In the following year, a second network consisting of 22 PCs, an AT file server, and four printers was added to the original system. These machines were placed in a single classroom to be used as an English writing lab and business word processing center. The library added more CDs, including the Readers Guide to Periodical Literature and a science index. And, the number of computer-capable teachers increased from the original 11 instructors to well over 40

* Source: "Queen Anne's QUCIN: A Successful Experiment in Educational Networking," by R.W. Lathroum & D.M. Chown, September 1988, THE Journal, IBM PC Special Issue.

(continued)

staff members, all of whom were proficient in basic applications programs, such as word processing and software in their own academic area.

By the third year, additional machines were added to the existing networks, including computers placed in eight vocational classrooms, a new business computer lab with 30 PS/2s, and a word processing lab in a ninth-grade classroom to permit all students to learn word processing in their first year of school.

Although the primary focus of the Queen Anne system was instructional, over the years, administrative applications increased as well. Initially, the network was used to record attendance and assemble a student database. Information was transmitted to an IBM S/34 mainframe at the central office via modem. In the second year, class schedules were automated and an electronic roll-taking system was installed that delivered phone messages to the homes of truant students. By the third year, computers were installed on the desks of every administrator, counselor, and secretary in the school. Report cards, transcripts, and discipline reports were added to the list of administrative functions handled by computers.

The Queen Anne experience shows how a network can grow over time, gradually adding new capabilities and capacity as demand and staff expertise increases. But, this is not the end of the story. The school is planning to add network access to every classroom, use modems to access on-line databases around the country, consolidate the programs and files residing on different file servers in the school networks, and expand the data transfer capabilities between the school and the school district mainframe system. Just imagine where Queen Anne will be in three more years!

peripherals from any computer in the network increases the flexibility of the system in terms of meeting staff, teacher, and student needs.

LAPTOP COMPUTERS

Another development that is as equally important as networking is the increasing popularity of laptop computers. Each year, portable computers get more powerful and less expensive. Indeed, the current generation of laptops have good legible screens, built-in hard disk drives and modems, and as much memory as most other personal computers. There are still major limitations on the duration of battery power and price. It is reasonable to predict that within a few years such computers will be available at commodity prices, and hence, affordable to many students and educators.

Ultimately, laptops are likely to have the kind of capabilities that we see on the more powerful workstations of today. This includes full multimedia display features, including video and sound and tremendous storage capability through a media, such as optical disk. We can also expect to see modems for laptops with cellular radio capabilities allowing connection to networks without the need for a phone jack. They are also likely to come in a variety of styles, colors, and materials to suit tastes and preferences.

Widespread ownership of laptop computers would change the computing picture significantly. Schools would no longer need to worry about how to provide computers for students and staff since they would be personal possessions, like watches or calculators. Many of the problems discussed in this book (e.g., location of machines, selection and buying hardware, security) would be irrelevant. Software would also likely become a personal purchase, much the same as books or school supplies. In many cases, programs may not actually be owned, but simply accessed on a networks when needed (like borrowing books from a library).

However, many considerations would still remain. Teachers would need to determine the best way to integrate computing into curricula, although they would have many more options than at present. All of the standard school administrative tasks (registration, attendance, testing, grade reporting, finance) would still need to be conducted, although the methods of collecting data might be quite different (e.g., downloading input from networks or individual laptops). Teachers would still need to be recruited, trained, and supervised, and school buildings would still need to be operated and maintained. The only difference is that all school activities would be computer-based in one form or another.

HYPERTEXT

In conjunction with major changes in hardware, there will also be a significant evolution of software. One of the more promising developments in the software world is hypermedia. Hypertext gives us a new way of organizing and accessing information in a nonlinear fashion. Any item of information, whether it is a single word, a sentence, a picture, or a video sequence, can be linked to any other item in a database. If you want to see the linked item, you simply select it. Thus, hypertext provides the capability to browse through a database in any order desired.

Hypertext capability is especially important as we move toward the availability and use of large databases. When you have the full *Encyclopedia Britannica, Oxford Dictionary* (unabridged), or works of Shakespeare on a single CD-ROM disk, it becomes difficult to easily navigate around so much information. The ability to move instantly from one concept to another makes this navigation much easier. Other hypertext capabilities include placing electronic bookmarks, seeing a record of what you have seen, and setting filters that block out information you are not interested in.

One particular hypertext system, HyperCard that runs on the Apple Macintosh computer, is becoming quite popular in schools. For example, Figure 9.1 shows a few screens from a high school yearbook which was done using HyperCard. HyperCard features an easy to use programming language (called HyperTalk) that allows teachers and students to develop their own hypertext "stacks." Furthermore, HyperCard can access videodisc and CD-ROM materials for multimedia presentations. Hypertext systems are available for other personal computers as well, and hypertext capabilities are likely to show up in all types of application programs (such as word processors) and online databases.[2]

ARTIFICIAL INTELLIGENCE

Another promising area of software development is artificial intelligence work. Artificial intelligence is a branch of computer science

---

[2] For an introduction to hypertext, see Barrett (1989) or Shneiderman and Kearsley (1989).

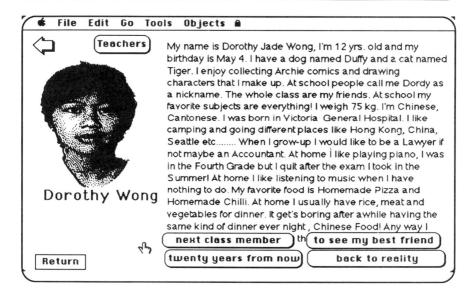

My name is Dorothy Jade Wong, I'm 12 yrs. old and my birthday is May 4. I have a dog named Duffy and a cat named Tiger. I enjoy collecting Archie comics and drawing characters that I make up. At school people call me Dordy as a nickname. The whole class are my friends. At school my favorite subjects are everything! I weigh 75 kg. I'm Chinese, Cantonese. I was born in Victoria General Hospital. I like camping and going different places like Hong Kong, China, Seattle etc........ When I grow-up I would like to be a Lawyer if not maybe an Accountant. At home I like playing piano, I was in the Fourth Grade but I quit after the exam I took in the Summer! At home I like listening to music when I have nothing to do. My favorite food is Homemade Pizza and Homemade Chilli. At home I usually have rice, meat and vegetables for dinner. It get's boring after awhile having the same kind of dinner ever night, Chinese Food! Any way I

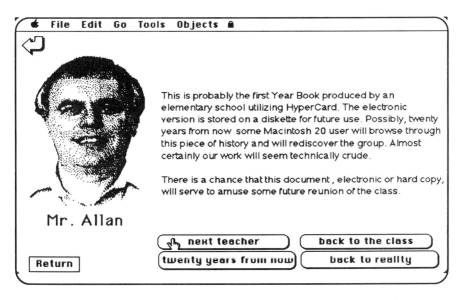

This is probably the first Year Book produced by an elementary school utilizing HyperCard. The electronic version is stored on a diskette for future use. Possibly, twenty years from now some Macintosh 20 user will browse through this piece of history and will rediscover the group. Almost certainly our work will seem technically crude.

There is a chance that this document, electronic or hard copy, will serve to amuse some future reunion of the class.

Figure 9.1. Screens from an Electronic Yearbook created using Hyper-Card® on an Apple Macintosh® (Credit: Apple Computer).

concerned with developing programs that can reason and make decisions. Programs with such capabilities can make computers behave in a more "intelligent" fashion than existing software which relies heavily on the user to make all choices.

Artificial intelligence methods could make all types of software easier to use. For example, it would be possible to use natural language or spoken instructions to have the computer accomplish a task ("Find the memo on fire drills and open it" or "Make a copy of that message and put it in my correspondence file"). More intelligence would also enable programs to understand what you are trying to do and provide better help when you get stuck. So, if you were trying to print out a document and it doesn't work, the computer could tell you why ("The printer is not turned on" or "You have the wrong file name"). In the case of administrative or financial software, smart versions of these programs would understand how one thing affects another and warn you when something isn't right or when you are about to make a mistake.

One important application area of artificial intelligence that has already received a lot of attention is expert systems. An expert system is a program that consists of the rules used by an expert to reach conclusions in a specific area. For example, expert systems are common in medicine to render diagnoses based upon the symptoms or test results shown by a patient. It would be possible to build expert systems for giving advice about how to best discipline a student, select a good teacher, or run a school. If experts exist who can make reliable decisions, their knowledge can be captured in an expert system.

Expert systems are starting to be used as learning tools in many classrooms. A special kind of authoring system, called an expert system shell, is used to create authoring system programs. Students can use these shells to build their own expert system for a class project. Alternatively, students can work with an existing expert system to solve case studies and exercises. In either case, students must understand the rules that are used to make decisions or judgments in a specific domain.

Another application of artificial intelligence to education is the development of intelligent tutoring systems. These are programs, like drills, tutorials, or simulations, that have a built-in advisor or coaching capability. When the student makes a mistake, they use diagnostic rules to determine what the student doesn't understand

and then provide an appropriate explanation. This makes such programs capable of very precise teaching. However, because of the incredible amount of detail required to create these programs, very few have been developed to date. This is likely to change over the next decade. Indeed, all forms of artificial intelligence software are likely to become more common.[3]

DISTANCE LEARNING

The schoolhouse model of education with a fixed schedule of classes has served us well for many centuries. However, it has some major deficiencies in terms of everyone having to learn the same thing in the same place at the same time. Almost every educator dreams of a system where students could progress at their own pace and learn when and where they wish. But such individualized instruction has never been feasible for cost and logistical reasons.

New technologies, such as computer networks and electronic conferencing systems, are making it increasingly possible to take education to the student instead of vice versa. Self-study courses have been available and used for many years with print and audiovisual materials. Without regular contact with an instructor and other students, however, such courses are not very successful, and most students drop out. When interactive media in the form of computer networking or two-way video conferencing is used as part of a course, distance learning is much more successful.

For example, using a computer network, a teacher can ask students to complete assignments and provide evaluative comments all via electronic mail. Class discussions can be carried out through conferences where everyone gets a chance to participate and see each other's responses. Students can interact with each other on projects using either electronic mail or through conferences. In addition, course materials could be available as online databases, or students could have access to commercial databases for class work. There are no geographical boundaries associated with such a class—students could be located anywhere.

---

[3] For further discussion of Artificial Intelligence and education, see Kearsley (1987) or Lawler and Yazdani (1987).

Many schools have already started to use a combination of television and telephone to provide distance learning. In many districts, there are too few students to justify a certain class at any particular school, but there may be enough students collectively at all schools. The class will be taught at one school and distributed via satellite, microwave, or cable to the other schools. Students at the "remote" sites can ask the teacher questions through the telephone connection and get their answer on the screen. This approach is an inexpensive way to share limited teaching resources and is a forerunner to full-scale two-way interactive video conferencing.

The administration of a distance learning program can be as comlicated (if not more so) as running a traditional school. A lot of the basic administrative data required, such as attendance (participation?), test scores, learning materials needed, or health records, can be best acquired electronically via telecommunications. Thus, even if distance learning activities don't involve the use of computer networks for student/teacher use, they may be highly desirable for administrative purposes.[4]

COMMUNITY OUTREACH

Related to the discussion of distance learning, but a distinct issue, is expanding the boundaries of the school to be more comprehensive in scope. Schools do not reach many students because they fail to deal with the constraints placed upon them by their family, home life, financial situation, or peer pressures. Furthermore, in many communities there is a large portion of adults that need basic education which could be provided by existing schools.

Teenage mothers, incarcerated juveniles, and the severely handicapped represent student populations that cannot be handled by the traditional school. Because of motivational or physical considerations, these students need a different sort of learning program. Computers can provide an alternative that works in the form of applications software, instructional programs, or networking. Most importantly, students can continue learning without having to go to school.

---

[4] Seer Bruder (1989) for a discussion of the issues involved in distance learning.

CROSS TOWN CULTURES

Picture two high schools in different parts of a city with two different student populations: Brownfield H.S. composed of mostly white kids whose parents are factory and clerical workers, and Southwest H.S. consisting primarily of black and hispanic kids with parents who work in service and retail jobs. The two schools are involved in a writing project that uses a bulletin board system available to all district schools. Students in English classes in both schools have been paired up at random and told to write a biography of their partner using information collected via electronic mail. They also exchanged photos which were then scanned in and added to a corner of the biography.

As the students exchanged messages and learned more about each other, they learned a lot about their corresponding neighborhoods. After completing the biographies, they decided to create a "living" map of the other school's part of town using HyperCard as a class project in Geography (the Geography teacher was not too sure about the idea but went along with it). First they drew a large-scale map marked off into rectangular sections. The students then formed small groups to work on the particular section that their electronic pen pal lives in. They made a bigger map of their section and drew symbols on the map representing homes, stores, and other places they have learned about.

While creating their maps, they continued to use the bulletin board system to correspond and get additional information needed. Some students wanted to known a little more about the area and buildings they were describing, so they went to the library and researched the history of the city. A few students made copies of old photos and scanned these into their maps. The History teacher was pleasantly surprised by the sudden interest in local history.

(continued)

Having finished their individual sections, they were all assembled together into one stack by the class computer whiz. When one section of the large map was selected, it was replaced by the more detailed map for that section. Selecting one of the symbols on this map brought up a window on the screen describing its significance. A lot of these windows had links to other symbols on the map that were related in some fashion.

Towards the end of the term, the students talked their teachers into taking field trips to each other's schools to share work and to see the pen pals and neighborhoods they have come to know so well.

Many students have a hostile home life that is not conducive to studying or school-related activities. Being able to use a computer in a school lab, library, or community center after school and on weekends can provide a way to get homework and projects done that would not otherwise be possible. Thus, the computer not only provides a tool to do better, but also a legitimate excuse to spend time on school work.

Carrying this idea one step further, computers located on or off the school site can be used to provide adult literacy programs. Again, the interactivity of the computer can be used to get reluctant learners into reading and writing activities that would be too boring or meaningless otherwise. As more and more communities have to cope with educating nonnative English speakers, the role of computer activities could become very important.

Another aspect of community outreach projects is to establish a close association with local businesses and industry. Computer activities can be offered to employees who need help in basic skills or completing high school (GED) qualifications. For many companies, such remedial programs are essential for retraining efforts, and they are happy to develop partnerships with schools. In many cases, they may provide support for computer equipment or resources needed.

Networks offer a number of advantages for outreach projects. They can provide access to a variety of programs and online databases without the need for a large software collection onsite. The use of electronic mail and bulletin board systems can extend the boundaries of a ghetto or rural areas and put participants in touch with others. Networks also make it easier to monitor usage and to evaluate how well the project is working.

These nontraditional forms of educational delivery present administrative challenges. In the case of off-site use of computers, there are security and maintenance problems to be solved. The use of telecommunications introduces the cost of phone lines. Teachers and school staff must be compensated fairly for their involvement in such efforts. Off-site support staff (often volunteers) must be trained. It is important that any school planning needed to conduct such community outreach activities already have considerable experience with computers in their own setting.

SUMMARY

We discussed new directions in technology and education that are likely to have significant impact on the future of computing in schools. This includes the effects of widespread use of networks and laptop computers, new software approaches, such as hypermedia and artificial intelligence, and emphasis on distance learning and community outreach efforts.

These developments are underway in many schools around the country. Networking is a logical next step once a school has acquired a number of computers. Laptops are beginning to show up in the hands of better-off colleges and university students. Hypertext and artificial intelligence software are being used in some classrooms. A number of schools are involved in distance learning or community outreach projects. In other words, these new developments are not way out in the future but already here.

EXERCISES

1. Identify how a network could be used for administratve purposes in a school district. If the network was national, how would this change the applications?

2. Investigate some of the commercial networks available for education. Which one do you feel has the most benefits?
3. Imagine that all the students, teachers, and staff in a school own their own laptop. Write out a scenario describing the daily use of computers in the school.
4. Examine a number of hypermedia systems and summarize their advantages and disadvantages for classroom use.
5. How would distance learning affect school funding and budgets? What would stay the same and what would be changed?
6. What factors would jeopardize the success of an off-site computer class, and how could these problems be prevented?

CHECKLIST FOR NEW DIRECTIONS

Networking

☐ Which type of network has the most promise for your schools?
☐ What additional planning and financial factors would networks introduce?

Laptop Computers

☐ What new policies and procedures for computer use would be needed with laptops?
☐ How would laptops change the economics of computer use in schools?

Hypertext

☐ What new capabilities does hypertext make possible?
☐ How important would hypertext be in school settings?

Artificial Intelligence

☐ What new capabilities does artificial intelligence software provide?
☐ How important would artificial intelligence be in school settings?

Distance Learning

☐ What new options does distance learning provide?

☐ What new administrative considerations would be introduced by distance learning activities?

Community Outreach

☐ What new options does community outreach provide?

☐ What new adminstrative considerations would be introduced by outreach activities using a computer?

10

Welcome to P.S. 1991

This chapter presents a hypothetical case study that follows Pat Sanchez, a new vice principal of P.S. 1991. Sanchez has just completed a Master's degree in Educational Administration with a focus on computers, and has four years experience as a teacher.

The case study takes the form of entries in a personal journal that chronicles Sanchez's experiences during the first school term. Sanchez was specifically hired to bring about changes in the school that would address problems such as poor student achievement, student discipline and attendance, teacher dissatisfaction, and administrative efficiency. Sanchez believes that computers can play an important part of the solution to some of these problems. Only those excerpts that have to do with computers are presented.

August 4

Today I got a call from Sandy Knight offering me the job at P.S. 1991. I was happy to get the offer and think I will take it. Seems like there is a real desire to do something there and they were pretty enthusiastic about my ideas on computer use. I told Sandy that I would like to think about the offer and let them know next week.

August 10

I called and let them know I would accept the job. I start in 2 weeks on the 24th. I guess I had better drive there this weekend and start looking for a place to live!

August 24

My first day on the job. A bit nervous in the morning but it wore off as the day went by. Moved into my office, met the staff, sat in on my first teacher's conference as a principal (very strange experience) and got a much more extensive tour of the school than during my interview.

After school, I went out and bought a new laptop PC and a good integrated package. I knew that I would be using the machine a lot and wanted something I could use at school or home easily. Besides, it was time to retire my old Apple II which had served me faithfully for 5 years!

August 26

Decided to get going on the computer stuff right away. I had an informal meeting with the office staff and asked them what they felt were the biggest problems running the office. They had a long list but the bottom line was lack of local control. They pass on all accounting, attendance, and grade information to the district, and then have a difficult time getting access to it. The office has a couple of Apple IIs that are used for word processing, but that is the extent of administrative computer use. They rely totally on the district for all data processing. No wonder they have problems!

After the meeting I called up the district DP director. She said that they had tried to put a terminal in some years ago, but the principal at that time didn't want it. I asked her how long it would take to get one installed. She said that they could have one there by the end of the week. What about training, I asked? She said they conduct a half-day overview workshop every other week. I scheduled myself and 2 staff members for the next workshop.

In the afternoon, I met with the 6 department heads and asked them about their computer needs. At the present time, there is a small lab of 4 Apple IIs used for some remedial activities using math and language drills and also by one math teacher for BASIC programming with the computer club. The department heads were pretty excited about the idea of getting more computers. They had all seen interesting projects at other schools and felt we should be using computers more at P.S. 1991. I found out that 2 teachers were currently working on their Master's degrees at a nearby university and taking educational computing courses. I asked the department heads to have a meeting with their teachers and find out what they think of using computers in their classroom and report back the results next week.

Sept 7

School started yesterday and it was a real zoo as usual. I'm glad I've been through this before—it gives you a much better perspective of what's important and what isn't. This morning we drove over to the district office and took the DP orientation session. The system is a real dinosaur and pretty cumbersome to use. Having access to it will help, but I can see that we are going to need to get our own system since the district doesn't plan on upgrading theirs in the near future. I asked the DP director what happened to our terminal and she explained that they had decided to buy us a PC clone instead of leasing a terminal. It should be delivered within a few days, she said. I inquired delicately if it was ok to use the machine for other things if we bought some software. She replied "Sure," blissfully unaware of what I had in mind.

Sept 9

I meet again today with the department heads and we discussed what their teachers had said about using computers. Most of the teachers were all for it and had lots of ideas, including recommendations for specific software and projects. Taking this as a positive sign, I asked each department head to write up a one-page description of these computer activities and hand it into me by the end of the week. They all groaned. I told them, "The journey of a thousand miles begins with a one page outline," and ajourned the meeting!

Tonight, there was a PTA meeting and I met some of the parents. I asked them what kinds of things they would like to see happen at the school. Quite a few of them mentioned computers. I hope they really meant it.

Sept 12

The PC showed up this morning and I had them install it in a common area in the main office. We all took turns signing on and calling up data. We had a brief meeting and worked out a tentative schedule for switching to online data entry instead of sending it over to the district office on forms. We also established some policies for who had what kind of access to the data. I explained the reports that I wanted to be run on a weekly and monthly basis.

In the afternoon, I spend some time kibitzing with the food services and building staff finding out what kinds of problems they have. It seems that they both could use some help keeping track of inventory, and I made a mental note to add that to my shopping list for administrative software. After going back to my office, I got out a recent issue of *THE Journal* and called some of the vendors of administrative packages to send me information about their programs. I didn't know exactly what I was looking for yet, but I figured it wouldn't hurt to start collecting information about alternatives.

Sept 15

Now that we have the PC in the office, I decided we should start using it for word processing and spreadsheets. I found enough money in the "miscellaneous administrative supplies" budget to buy a copy of the integrated package I use on my machine and a good printer. As soon as everyone gets used to it, we can stop using the Apples and move them into the lab. I know the teachers will appreciate the extra machines.

By the end of the day, all of the department heads had handed in their computing outlines—a small victory. This weekend I will take their input and fashion it into a computer plan. With a little luck, I will be able to take a final version to the school board by the end of the month.

Sept 18

Finished the computer plan. It was a lot of work. I proposed we get a few more PCs for the office with a hard disk for keeping student records, a laser printer, and an OCR scanner. I figure we can use the scanner for attendance, grading, and test scoring, and save a lot of time processing data. I would like to put a machine in the food services and staff lounge too, but that's a bit too ambitious for a start.

I also proposed that we enlarge and upgrade the Apple II lab to have 16 machines and a large collection of software that would address the various ideas proposed by the teachers. I suggested that we hire a full-time lab coordinator to work with the teachers and their students. I decided to go with the lab approach to avoid the problem of putting machines in some classrooms and not others. While I believe the classroom is probably the best place to put them, it just isn't a good political step. I did propose a couple of additional machines on carts with LCD panels that teachers could schedule for use in their classrooms, so this should help.

Recommending we buy PCs for the office and Apple IIs for the lab was a difficult choice since it means there will be no compatibility between the two groups of machines. However, the PCs make sense because of the administrative software available and their cost; the Apple IIs make sense from an educational software perspective and the fact that there are already two teachers comfortable with them. Besides, I can take care of the compatibility problems later with a network that lets different machines talk to each other.

There were lots of other things I wanted to propose, like some modems and a bulletin board system or CD-ROM player, but I decided it would be better to start off modestly. It will be tough enough getting all this through!

I am going to have about 50 copies of the plan made up and then circulate it to all staff, to the superintendent and board members, and to the PTA officers. This should start the fireworks!

Sept 23

Whew, it's been busy! I asked the department heads at this week's meeting to solicit comments from their teachers on the computer plan and be ready to summarize it at next week's meeting. I asked them for their initial reactions—they were generally positive, but I don't think most of them had actually read it yet. They probably don't expect much to come of it; they will take it a bit more seriously once it starts to happen.

I also summarized the report at this week's staff meeting. The only real objection anyone had was where the money was going to come from. I told people not to worry about that—since I don't have a clue at this point, I couldn't provide much of an answer! I scheduled a meeting with the PTA officers next week to go over the plan with them. I think the PTA is going to be the key to getting funding; if I can get strong support from the parents, I will have the benefit of grassroots support when I go before the board.

Sept 29

Met with PTA committee last night and got their ok to make a presentation at next month's meeting (which is two weeks away). This will give me a chance to try out my presentation with the parents before I give it to the board later in the month. While the goal of the PTA presentation is only to win their approval, I would like to get them to make some kind of commitment if possible. Perhaps, I could get them to simply sign a letter of support or something.

Oct 11

The PTA presentation on the computer plan went much better than I had expected. It was partly a matter of timing—my presentation came after a talk on drug programs which got everyone pretty worked up. I think some of the adrenaline was left over for my talk. I told parents that I believed the significant use of computers in the classroom would get their kids more interested in school and improve their involvement in classes. Their response was: "What are we waiting for?" I explained that this was going to cost additional money for computers, software, and the extra staff needed. A couple of parents said that they would rather have money spent on computers than a lot of the other things that it got wasted on.

But the best thing to come out of the meeting was a parent named Suzanne Levy who came up and introduced herself after the meeting. She explained that her husband had been asked by his company to investigate the use of the computer to teach basic skills to adults, and she wondered if I knew anything about these programs. Apparently, the company had a lot of non-English-speaking workers who needed help with writing, reading, and basic math, and the company was looking for a solution. As luck would have it, I had done a term paper on this as part of my MA and knew something about it. The next morning, I called Jon Levy and introduced myself. I answered a lot of his questions and he asked me if I could show him some examples of the kind of programs I was talking about. I told him that I didn't have any at the school, but I would try to set something up and call him back. When I hung up the phone, I knew that this was a good opportunity, although at the time, I didn't know how important it would turn out to be.

Oct 14

I decided the best strategy for finding the kind of basic skills software that Jon Levy was interested in was to rely on a vendor with experience in this area. From the study I had done in college, I had the names and addresses of the companies and called up a few. One of the companies had a representative in a nearby city who was willing to come out and give a demo if I could provide the machines. Their software resided on a hard disk and could work with Apple IIs. I went ahead and called Jon and set up a presentation at the school for the day the rep could come. I hoped that the vendor rep would show up and have a good demo!

Oct 17

I presented my computer plan to the board tonight. They are going to be a tough bunch to sell. They had no objections to the plan itself, but categorically ruled out using any money from this year's budget. I tried to steer them away from the financing issue and focus on the benefits. They were a lot more sympathetic to the administrative part of the proposal than the lab, so I spent most of my time on that. I got them to agree to attend a demo of the scanner at the school if I could arrange one. Felt kind of discouraged after the meeting but I reminded myself that nothing worthwhile ever comes easy! Tomorrow, I will call some of the scanner companies and see if I can get someone to come and give me a demo.

Oct 24

We had the demo for Jon Levy this afternoon and it went very well. The rep knew her stuff and the software was really good. Jon asked if I could arrange another demo in a week or so. He wanted to bring back his boss and some employees to try out the programs. The rep was willing so we agreed to do it. After the demo, I told Jon about an idea that I had. If his company would be willing to buy the hardware and software needed, the school would provide the lab and teachers to supervise employees using the machines in the evenings and weekends. I pointed out that the machines would be a donation so his company could probably get a tax break out of it, as well as have certified teachers available at no cost to the company. He said it was an interesting idea and he would talk to his boss about it. The idea had just occurred to me earlier in the day when I was puzzling about how to get the equipment needed without any money. I was out on a limb proposing that teachers would be willing to supervise in the lab, but I had an intuition this would work somehow.

Oct 27

I spent about an hour this morning trying to find a scanner company that would do a demo. No luck. However, one company had a videotape that they claimed would do the job, so I asked them to send it to me. I also spent some time with the office staff estimating how long it took to do various tasks that we could use the scanner for. I then made up a comparison chart that showed how much time we could save using the scanner and the payoffs in terms of handling more work with the same staff level. I knew that staff increases were a sensitive issue with the board and thought that this might be an effective strategy to sell the administrative system to them.

In the afternoon I got a break from an unexpected source. I happened to call the district DP coordinator to check on file formats

and get a preliminary reading on her feeling about us doing some of
our own processing. It turns out that the district was interested in
exploring this in order to see if it would decrease their workload.
They had budgeted some money to put a system into one school as
an experiment, but had not picked a school yet. I said: "We volunteer!" She said that if our board requested the equipment, the district would provide it. Now I had something quite specific to ask
the board.

Oct 29

Today we did the demo for Jon Levy and his boss. He brought along
a couple of employees who would be eligible for the program, and
they worked with the software for about half an hour while Jon, his
boss, and I discussed the idea of having the basic skills instruction
done at the school. When we went back to the lab to check on the
two employees, they were totally absorbed in the programs. When
asked what they thought of it, they smiled and said they liked it.
That was all it took—the smiles on the faces of those two employees.
Jon's boss looked at me and asked how quickly I could have a proposal written for the project. "Would two days be soon enough," I
asked? Needless to say, I was pretty excited.

Oct 31

I dropped off the basic skills proposal on my way to school today,
having stayed up till about 2 am getting it done. I had a meeting
yesterday with the heads of the math and language arts department
and cleared the idea with them. Since I didn't have any money to
pay the teachers for their participation, I used the leverage I did
have—career advancement credits and comp time. I knew that
eventually real compensation would be needed, but I was sure that
we would find a source for the extra money if the program got off
the ground and was successful.

I called and scheduled a presentation at the next board meeting.
I planned to make my pitch for the administrative system, including
the video, my comparison study, and the offer from the district for
the equipment. I also thought that I had better brief them on the

basic skills proposal, regardless of how it turned out. It was important that they should know what I'm up to.

Nov 4

Got a call from Jon Levy today saying that the company liked the idea and wanted to go ahead with it. He would be the company liaison for the project. I told him that I had still had to sell it to the school board. I couldn't believe my luck! I was going to walk into my second board meeting with the news that people were waiting in the wings to give us the equipment that I had merely proposed last month.

There was still one sticky point, though. I still needed money for the computer coordinator and lab supervisor. I knew that the lab would not fly without these people (and good ones at that). I also suspected that I would not be able to get the money out of the budget, given the clear-cut position of the board. I decided that I had only one alternative—turn an existing teaching position into the computer coordinator job, and rely on volunteer aides for the lab assistant. However, to do this I would have to have the support of the teachers, and moreover, a specific position available.

I asked the department heads to meet with me at the end of the day and told them the good news about the basic skills project. I explained that they would be able to use the machines during the day as they wished, and also that I was going to order the software they had requested out of the supplies budget. I joked that they could forget ordering chalk or erasers for the rest of the year. Everyone was pretty happy about the news. I shared with them the last obstacle that I needed to clear up before presenting the whole thing to the board, and asked them for their help.

We brainstormed for a while and then someone suggested that maybe we could use an existing teaching position. I asked if anyone had any ideas about any specific teachers who might not want to continue teaching. After a long silence, one of the heads said that he had a teacher who had been talking a lot about retiring lately. I said I would talk to her tomorrow. Clearly, the idea of taking away a teaching position had made everyone tense—it was not a popular idea.

Nov 10

We had the board meeting and much to my relief, everything went well. The board members liked the idea of a collaborative project with a local company, and also liked the idea of "helping" out the district with the administrative system. I was candid about the fact that I did not have all the pieces worked out, especially the staffing of the lab (the teacher was not really ready to retire yet). They unanimously approved my computer plan. As long as I could get things free and didn't need to dip into the budget, they were happy to let me get on with it. Of course, I knew that next year's budget would need to cover a lot of computing expenses, but I figured that I would worry about that bridge when the time came to cross it.

Nov 11

Called up Jon Levy and told him that the board had approved the idea and we could go ahead with the basic skills project. He said he would make up the purchase order and have the hardware and software ordered as soon as possible. I asked him to order the hardware through the local dealer, and to be sure that a service contract was included. Since we had no budget for maintenance of the machines, I knew that without such a service contract we would be in trouble.

The basic skills software was to be ordered from the vendor who had made the demonstrations. I felt a little uneasy about selecting that particular software without conducting a more comprehensive evaluation; on the other hand, the rep had provided a copy of a journal article that compared basic skills packages, and theirs came out pretty good. I had also talked to a couple of other schools who were using the package, and they seemed happy with it. Besides, the rep was knowledgeable and I felt that we would get good support. The contract included 10 hours of initial training and ongoing consultation, and more time could be purchased if needed.

After talking to Jon, I called up the district coordinator and told her that the board had approved the idea of using our school as a test site for the scanner and administrative system. The superintendent would be sending her a memo formalizing the request in a day or so. She said she would go ahead and put in the purchase order for the equipment and software I requested. Selecting the software was easy—the same package that the scanner company had shown in their videotape happened to be the one that I had decided would best meet our needs. The only catch was that the company did not provide any live training—only videos. I hope the tapes are good!

Nov 12

Spent most of the morning with the building supervisor trying to figure out what to do with the lab. There was clearly no way to add anything more to the existing lab, so we had to find some new space. Any kind of building renovations were out of the question, due to red tape and time considerations. We went around the school looking for unused space, but there was nothing. I knew that any attempt to usurp an existing room would be political dynamite, and wanted to avoid that at all costs. Finally, we stumbled across a possibility— an old room used to store athletic equipment. It was big enough, although it had no windows. With some work, it would do. Could I sell the idea to the phys-ed staff? I went to see the phys-ed department head. I asked him if he was happy with the athletic storage situation. It turns out he wasn't. He said what he really needed was something outside, closer to the field. I asked him if he would like a nice new shed. And so, we had space for our new computer lab. I asked the building super to make up some plans for refurbishing the new lab and building a shed for the athletics department. This was going to take some creative juggling of the budget, but I was confident I could find the money somewhere in the "miscellaneous building expenses" accounts.

Nov 15

Went to the PTA meeting tonight and made a brief presentation on the new lab, and what kind of new computer activities we would be trying out next term. I had asked Jon Levy to attend, and he gave a brief explanation of his company's basic skills program. Then I outlined my plan for volunteer aides to work a half day a week, and we passed out a sign-out sheet. It came back full with a new page attached—a waiting list! Maybe it was the promise of getting free computer training on Sats. that helped. Now, if I could just solve the coordinator problem, we would be ready to roll. On the way home, I resolved to meet with the department heads again tomorrow and see if we could come up with something.

Nov 16

I met with the department heads in the afternoon after school and updated them on the progress of the basic skills lab. I told them about the parents' enthusiastic response to the call for volunteer computer aides, and also about the plan to use the old storage area for the new lab. Everyone agreed that the storage area would need a lot of work to make it a pleasant place to work; I assured them that they wouldn't recognize it by the time the remodeling was done. I sure hoped what I was telling them would come true!

Then we got down to the computer coordinator issue. I asked if anyone had any new ideas. Nobody did. So I proposed my own. I asked if they thought any of their teachers would be interested in taking the job of computer coordinator next term. Two teachers (the two who were completing their Master's degrees in educational computing) were nominated. I then asked if it was possible for other teachers to share the load if we made one of those teachers the computer coordinator. They would be compensated the same way as the teachers participating in the basic skills program. There was some grumbling about extra work loads, but the discussion quickly turned to how they could work out the scheduling. By the end of the meeting, they had agreed to the plan, provided that it was acceptable to all the teachers involved. I asked them to talk it over with their teachers and let me know if they were agreeable. I also said I would talk to the two teachers proposed for the coordinator job tomorrow.

Nov 17

I talked to the two teachers at lunch break and explained what would be involved in the coordinator job. I was also careful to explain that it would only be for one term and that we would probably hire someone permanent during the summer. They were both interested in the job, but one of them was more enthusiastic about it than the other, and by the end of lunch had convinced us both to let her try it. She agreed not only to supervise the day use of the lab, but also to coordinate the basic skills project activities in the evening and weekends.

I had some misgivings about letting someone without any real experience fill the coordinator role. Without the experience, she would likely make some mistakes that would jeopardize the success of the computer projects. On the other hand, she had lots of enthusiasm and this counts for a lot! Anyway, I didn't really have any other options so this approach would have to work.

Nov 26

The scanner finally arrived today. The computers and software arrived last week, and we set everything up and played around a little. Tomorrow, we will sit down and watch the first two training tapes, and then see if we can get the system working. I expect it will take us a few weeks to get the hang of it. I would like to start using the system at the beginning of next term, and so we need to make some trial runs before the end of this year.

The new lab is coming along. Unfortunately, the shed is not done yet so we can't move all the athletic gear out of the room to work. New lights and power outlets have been installed, and the tables will go in as soon as the room is cleaned out, painted, and the new carpet installed. The computers should arrive anyday now; I have asked the dealer to hang on to them until we are ready for them. This is all pretty hectic!

Dec 9

Having a lot of problems getting the scanner to work, as well as learning how to use the administrative software. The training tapes are ok, but they don't answer all of the questions we have. I think the rep is getting tired of us calling every day.

The machines for the lab are at the dealer waiting for the lab to get finished. Still waiting for the athletic shed to get done so we can get everything out of the room and finish it. I'm beginning to have my doubts about whether the lab will be ready for next term, but I'm keeping them to myself.

Today I finished the draft budget for next year. It includes money for more software and salaries for the computer coordinator and lab assistant. If things go ok next term, there shouldn't be any problem convincing the board that the cost will be worth it.

Dec 14

Yesterday, we made a field trip to another school in the city that uses the same administrative software and scanner we bought. This was our reps idea, and it worked great. We finally got some answers to our questions and got to see how things were supposed to work. Using what we learned yesterday, we were able to get things working fairly well this morning, and I think we will be able to make a test run on attendance and grading next week—just in time before Christmas break!

We also had a breakthrough of sorts on the lab. The athletic shed finally got completed enough to move everything into it. Now the work on the lab can be finished. The building super said he thinks he can get it ready by the end of December, in time to set things up for the first week of class next term.

I decided that instead of the machines just sitting in storage at the dealers, we might as well put them to use. I announced to the teachers that anyone who wanted could take a machine home over the holidays to practice with the new software. The teachers said that this was a sneaky way to get them to work during their vacation, but many of them requested machines. They were right—it was a sneaky plan—but probably the best way to get them comfortable with the machines before next term. I just hope I can get them to bring the machines back to school to put in the lab when it is finally ready!

Dec 19

We ran this week's attendance and grades through the system, and things seem to work ok. We have most of the student database created, and we are amusing ourselves running all kinds of crazy online searches. Looks like the system will be ready for use next term.

The lab is coming along. It has now been painted and the carpet was put down this morning. It looks great. The tables and cabinets will be put in the week after Christmas, so we should be able to move the equipment in the week before classes start. Things will certainly be busy next term with so much going on.

Today, I was sitting in my office after school thinking about my first term. I didn't do too badly on the computer front, thanks to some lucky breaks. Of course, the real fun starts next term when we try and make all of this stuff work. I have to count on my teachers to do a good job with the computers in their classrooms. They will need a lot of guidance and support. I wonder if my new computer coordinator can pull this off? I also have to show that the new administrative software can produce all the benefits I promised.

Yes, the real challenge lies ahead. I'm looking forward to it.

EXERCISES

1. Sanchez credits luck for the success achieved. Was it just a matter of luck? What do you think would have happened without the "lucky breaks"?

2. P.S. 1991 does not have any union representation. How would things have been different if there had been union involvement?

3. Do you agree with all the actions taken by Sanchez? What decisions or actions would you have done differently? How would it have changed things?

4. Can you think of anything important that Sanchez did not deal with (so far)? What are the possible consequences of this omission?

5. Do you think Sanchez moved too fast in getting more computers into the school? Would it have been better to have just focused on the administrative or classroom applications one at a time? What are the consequences of moving too fast or too slow when introducing computers?

Glossary

Applications software   Programs that perform general tasks, such as word processing, spreadsheets, databases, etc.

Artificial Intelligence   A branch of computer science dedicated to the development of programs that can think and reason.

ASCII (American Standard Code for Information Interchange)   A standard format for computer files (pronounced "ask-key").

Authoring languages   Computer languages specially designed for creating instructional software.

Backing up   To make a copy of a file or program in case the original gets damaged or lost.

BASIC   A computer programming language designed for beginners that is very popular on personal computers.

Baud   A measure of transmission speed used in telecommunications. Approximately the same as characters per second (i.e., 1200 baud = 1200 cps).

Boot   The step of getting a computer to load an initial program and start processing (short for "bootstrap").

143

Bulletin Boards   Use of a computer network to exchange information in a public forum (contrasts with electronic mail in which messages are private).

Bug   A mistake in a computer program.

Byte   The basic unit of computer storage. A byte is approximately equal to one character of text. A kilobyte = 1,000 bytes; a megabyte = 1 million bytes.

CPU (Central Processing Unit)   The main memory and processing component of a computer.

Chip   A small piece of silicon containing electronic circuits.

Circuit Card   A small board that contains chips which provide memory or processing functions. Comprise the CPU.

Courseware   Curriculum-based software.

Cursor   An indicator on the display screen that shows the current input location.

Data processing   Use of computers for administrative or financial tasks.

Disk drive   A device that reads and writes data onto disks.

Distributed processing   Sharing of data and processing tasks across multiple machines in a network.

DOS (Disk Operating System)   The operating system used on IBM PCs and compatibles.

Files   Information shared on disks.

Hard disk   A disk drive that contains an unremovable disk.

Hardware   The physical components of a computer system (e.g., display monitor, printer, disk drives).

Interactivity Feedback provided to a user response.

Local Area Network (LAN) A network that connects computers located in the same building using cables.

Liquid Crystal Display (LCD) A type of computer display that is flat and uses very little power.

Mainframe A large computer system.

Menu A list of options or files that the user can select in a program.

Microcomputer A small computer that can fit on a desk. Also called a personal computer.

Minicomputer A medium-sized computer designed to be used by multiple users at once.

Modem A device that lets a computer send and receive information via telephone lines.

Mouse A handheld device used to move the cursor on the screen.

Operating system The software that manages the computer (e.g., DOS, Unix).

Peripherals Hardware other than the CPU, including all input and output devices (e.g., keyboards, mouse, printers), and storage devices (disk drives).

Pixels A single addressable point on a display, and a measure of screen resolution.

Program A set of instructions that makes the computer do something. Same as software.

RAM (Random Access Memory) The temporary storage area of the CPU where data and programs are kept during processing. Once the computer is turned off, RAM is erased; hence, the need to store information on disks.

ROM (Read Only Memory)   A permanent storage area of the CPU where some operating system programs are stored. ROM cannot be changed by the user.

Software   Sets of instructions that make the computer do something. Same as program.

Serial interface   A connector used to connect printers or modems to a CPU.

Terminal   A display and keyboard without a CPU or disk drives. Used on networks to send/receive data.

Timesharing   The sharing of a mainframe or minicomputer by many users at the same time.

UNIX   An operating system common on minicomputers and work stations.

Utility programs   Small programs that perform very specific tasks (such as making labels, grammar checkers, appointment calendars.

Windows   The ability to overlap information in different areas on a display screen.

References

Allessi, S., & Trollip, S. (1985). *Computer based instruction: Methods and development.* Englewood Cliffs, NJ: Prentice-Hall.

Baker, F.B. (1978). *Computer-managed instruction: Theory and practice.* Englewood Cliffs, NJ: Educational Technology Publications.

Bank, A., & Williams, R.C. (1987). *Information systems and school improvement: Inventing the future.* New York: Teacher's College Press.

Barrett, E. (1989). *The society of text.* Cambridge, MA: MIT Press.

Beach, R.H., & Lindahl, R.A. (1984). The hidden costs of training your staff. *Electronic Learning, 3*(7), 30.

Bennett, R.H. (1981). Humanizing student scheduling. *NASSP Bulletin, 65*(443), 120–121.

Bluhm, H. (1987). *Administrative uses of computers in the schools.* Englewood Cliffs, NJ: Prentice-Hall.

Bork, A. (1985). *Personal computers for education.* New York: Harper & Row.

Brady, H. (1985). School districts singled out on piracy charges. *Classroom Computer Learning, 6*(2), 14.

Bruder, I. (1989, April). Distance learning. *Electronic Learning,* pp. 30–35.

Budoff, M., Thorman, J., & Gras, A. (1984). *Microcomputers in special education.* Cambridge, MA: Brookline Books.

Case, C.M. (1969). The application of PERT to large-scale educational research and evaluation studies. *Educational Technology, 9*(10).

Cheever, D.S. (1986). *School administrator's guide to computers in education.* Reading, MA: Addison-Wesley.

Church, G.D., & Bender, M. (1985). School administration and technology: Planning educational roles. *Educational Technology, 25*(6), 21–24.

Coburn, P. et al. (1985). *Practical guide to computers in education.* Reading, MA: Addison-Wesley, 1985.

Collis, B. (1988). *Computers, curriculum, and whole class instruction: Issues and ideas.* Belmont, CA: Wadsworth.

Daiute, C. (1985). *Writing and computers.* Reading, MA: Addison-Wesley.

Dembowski, F.L. (1984). The microcomputer and transportation. *School Business Affairs, 50*(5), 14.

Fisher, G., & Finkel, L. (1984). The computer lab: Where it helps and where it doesn't. *Electronic Learning, 4*(2), 52.

Forman, K. (1983). Networking saves $$ for New York school district. *Electronic Education, 3*(1), 62–63.

Glossbrenner, A. (1983). *The complete handbook of personal computer communications.* New York: St. Martins Press.

Goldenberg, E.P., Russell, S., & Carter, C. (1984). *Computers, education, and special needs.* Reading, MA: Addison-Wesley.

Goodson, B. (1984). Software report: Are computer managed instruction programs worth the trouble? *Electronic Learning, 4*(1), 8.

Guilbeau, J.J. (1984). Micros for the special education administrator: A Louisiana district's network of special educators. *Electronic Learning, 3*(5), 43.

Gustafson, T.J. (1985). *Microcomputers and educational administration.* Englewood Cliffs, NJ: Prentice-Hall.

Hai, D.M. (1975). PERT in higher education. *Educational Technology, 15*(10).

Hannifin, M.J., & Peck, K. (1988). *The design, development and evaluation of instructional software.* New York: Macmillan.

Hertz, R. (1986). *Computers in the language classroom.* Reading, MA: Addison-Wesley.

Hill, F. (1988). *Tomorrow's learning environment: Planning for technology.* Alexandria, VA: NSBA Institute for the Transfer of Technology to Education.

Hoover, T., & Gould, S. (1982). Computerizing the school office: The hidden cost. *NASSP Bulletin, 66*(445), 89–91.

Hunter, B. (1984). *My students use computers.* Reston, VA: Reston Publishing Co.

Jamison, D. et al. (1975). How effective is CAI? A review of the research. *Educational Leadership, 33,* 41–55.

Kacanek, P. (1984). Spreadsheets and pupil enrollment projections. *Electronic Learning, 4*(2), 26–28.

Kearsley, G. (1982). *Costs, benefits and productivity in training systems.* Reading, MA: Addison-Wesley.

Kearsley, G. (1986). *Authoring: The design of instructional software.* Reading, MA: Addison-Wesley.

Kearsley, G. (1987). *Artificial intelligence and instruction.* Reading, MA: Addison-Wesley.

Krahn, K., & Hughes, B. (1976). Benefits of computer class scheduling. *NASSP Bulletin, 60*(396), 106–108.

Kulick, J.A., Bangert, R.L., & Williams, G.W. (1983). Effects of computer-based teaching on secondary school students. *Journal of Educational Psychology, 75,* 46–54.

Lathrop, A., & Goodson, B. (1984). *Courseware in the classroom.* Reading, MA: Addison-Wesley.

Lawler, R., & Yazdani, M. (1987). *Artificial intelligence and education* (Vol. 1). Norwood, NJ: Ablex.

Miller, H. (1988). *An administrator's manual for the use of microcomputers in the schools.* Englewood Cliffs, NJ: Prentice-Hall.

Niemiec, R., & Walberg, H. (1987). Comparative effects of computer assisted instruction: A synthesis of reviews. *Journal of Educational Computing Research, 3*(1), 19–37.

Papert, S. (1980). *Mindstorms: Children, computers and powerful ideas.* New York: Basic Books.

Pennington, J.R. (1984). Word processing and teacher evaluation. *Electronic Learning, 3*(6), 66–68.

Perelman, L. (1987). *Technology and transformation of schools.* Alexandria, VA: NSBA Institute for the Transfer of Technology to Education.

Pogrow, S. (1983). *Education in the computer age: Issues of policy, practice and reform.* Beverly Hills, CA: Sage Publications.

Pogrow, S. (1984). Finance packages for the central district office. *Electronic Learning, 2*(8), 32–36.

Pogrow, S. (1985). The state-of-the-art in educational administration software. *THE Journal, 13*(4), 72–74.

Radin, S., & Greensberg, H.M. (1983). *Computer literacy for school administrators and supervisors.* Lexington, MA: D.C. Heath.

Riesdesel, C.A., & Clements, D.H. (1985). *Coping with computers in the elementary and middle school.* Englewood Cliffs, NJ: Prentice-Hall.

Roberts, N. (1983). *Introduction to computer simulation.* Reading, MA: Addison-Wesley.

Roberts, N., Carter, R., Fricl, S., & Miller, M. (1988). *Integrating computers into the elementary and middle school.* Englewood Cliffs, NJ: Prentice-Hall.

Roblyer, M.D. (1988). The effectiveness of microcomputers in education: A review of the research from 1980–1987. *THE Journal, 88.*

Shneiderman, B., & Kearsley, G. (1989). *Hypertext hands-on!* Reading, MA: Addison-Wesley.

Smith, R., & Kauffman, D. (1985). Before you choose a network, consider... *Electronic Education, 4*(6), 25–28.

Snyder, T., & Palmer, J. (1986). *In search of the most amazing thing: Children, education and computers.* Reading, MA: Addison-Wesley.

Stronge, J.H., & Turner, J.H. (1983). Computer scheduling: Is it worth the effort? *Electronic Education, 3*(1), 57.

Turban, E. (1988). Decision support systems in academic administration. *Journal of Educational Administration, 26*(1), 97–113.

Turner, S., & Land, M. (1988). *Tools for schools: Applications software for the classroom.* Belmont, CA: Wadsworth.

U.S. Congress, Office of Technology Assessment. (1988). *Power on! New tools for teaching and learning.* Washington, DC: GPO. [OTA-SET-379]

Wagner, L. (1982). *The economics of educational media.* New York: St. Martins Press.

Watt, M., & Watt, D. (1986). *Teaching with Logo: Building blocks for learning.* Reading, MA: Addison-Wesley.

White, G.T. (1984). Micros for the special educator: How to use a computer to keep up with special education law. *Electronic Learning, 3*(5), 29–40.

Williams, F., & Williams, V. (1984). *Microcomputers in elementary education.* Belmont, CA: Wadsworth.

Williams, W.L., & LeCesne, T. (1985). Getting the picture: Graphs and charts by computer. *Electronic Learning, 4*(5), 40–44.

Willis, J., Hovey, L., & Hovey, K. (1987). *Computer simulations: A sourcebook to learning in an electronic environment.* New York: Garland Publishing.

Wresch, W. (1988, April). Six directions for computer analysis of student writing. *The Computing Teacher.*

Wright, E., & Forcier, R.C. (1985). *The computer: A tool for the teacher.* Belmont, CA: Wadsworth.

Appendix
Further Resources

This book only provides an introduction to the topic of administrative computing. To get more deeply involved, you need to read more, talk to other administrators who have computer experience, and attend conferences. This must be an ongoing activity since things change continuously in the computer field. Periodicals are a good source of up-to-date information about hardware and software, as well as for who is doing what in the educational computing field.

The list below identifies some important resources that should help you find out more about computer applications. All of the organizations listed have special reports or subgroups dealing with technology in schools, and you will also find relevant articles in their journals or newsletters. The periodicals listed specialize in educational computing, and are a very good source of up-to-date information about the field. The networks identified are all specifically for educational use. Finally, the books listed in the references are also important sources for further information.

ORGANIZATIONS
(Including their journals/newsletters)

Association for Supervision and Curriculum Development
125 North West St.
Alexandria, VA 22314
703/549-9110

Center for Special Education Technology
1920 Association Dr.
Reston, VA 22091
703/620-3660

International Society for Technology in Education (ISTE)
University of Oregon
1787 Agate St.
Eugene, OR 97403
503/686-4414
The Computing Teacher; Education Administrators SIG Bulletin

Computer Using Educators of California
P.O. Box 18547
San Jose, CA 95158
408/244-2559
CUE Newsletter

Assoc. for Educational Communications and Technology
1126 Sixteenth St., N.W.
Washington, DC 20036
202/466-4780
Educational Communication and Technology Journal; Tech Trends

Educational Products Information Exchange
P.O. Box 839
Water Mill, NY 11976
516/283-4922
EPIEgram

Minnesota Educational Computing Corporation
2520 Broadway Dr.
St. Paul, MN 55113
612/638-0600
MECC Newsletter

National Association of Secondary School Principals
1904 Association Dr.
Reston, VA 22091
703/860-0200
NASSP Bulletin; School Tech News

National Association of Independent Schools
18 Tremont St.
Boston, MA 02108
617/723-6900

National Association of Elementary School Principals
1615 Duke St.
Alexandria, VA 22314
703/684-3345
Principal

National Education Association
1201 16th St., N.W.
Washington, DC
202/822-7200

Resources in Computer Education (RICE)
Northwest Regional Educational Lab
300 SW 6th Ave.
Portland, OR 97204
503/248-6300

American Association of School Administrators
1801 North Moore St.
Arlington, VA 22209
703/528-0700
The School Administrator

Association of School Business Officials
11401 North Shore Dr.
Reston, VA 22090
703/478-0405
School Business Affairs

Institute for the Transfer of Technology to Education (ITTE)
National School Boards Association
1680 Duke St.
Alexandria, VA 22314
703/838-6722

PERIODICALS

Classroom Computer Learning
Peter Li, Inc.
19 Davis Dr.
Belmont, CA 94002
415/592-7810

Collegiate Microcomputer
Rose-Hulman Institute of Technology
Terre Haute, In 47803
812/877-1511

Educational Technology
140 Sylvan Ave.
Englewood Cliffs, NJ 07632
201/871-4007

Electronic Education
Electronic Communications, Inc.
1311 Executive Dr., Suite 2201
Tallahassee, FL 32301
904/878-4178

Electronic Learning
Teaching and Computers
Scholastic Learning
730 Broadway
New York, NY 10003
212/505-3000

T.H.E. Journal
Information Synergy Inc.
P.O. Box 15126
Santa Ana, CA 92705
714/261-0366

NETWORKS

EINSTEIN
Learning Link
356 W. 58th St.
New York, NY 10019
212/560-6613

KIDNET
National Geographic Kids Network
National Geographic Society
Washington, DC 20036
202/775-6580

MIX
McGraw-Hill Information Network
P.O. Box 382
Northfield, MN 55057
503/345-8527

FrEdMail
c/o Al Rogers
4021 Allen School Rd.
Bonita, CA 92002

AT&T Long Distance Learning Network
AT&T
P.O. Box 716
Basking Ridge, NJ 07920-0716
619/943-1314

SPECIALNET
National Assoc. of State Directors of Special Education
2021 K. St., Suite 315
Washington, DC 20006
202/296-1800

BITNET
Educom
777 Alexander Rd.
Princeton, NJ 08540
609/520-3340

BRS/Educator
1200 Rt 7
Latham, NY 12110
518/783-1161

Author Index

A

Allessi, S., 66, *147*

B

Baker, F.B., 52, *147*
Bangert, R.L., 48, *149*
Bank, A., 22, 85, *147*
Barrett, E., 116, *147*
Beach, R.H., 78, *147*
Bender, M., 25, *147*
Bennett, R.H., 17, *147*
Bluhm, H., 2, *147*
Bork, A., 43, *147*
Brady, H., 65, *147*
Bruder, I., 120, *147*
Budhoff, M., 48, *147*

C

Carter, C., 48, *148*
Carter, R., 7, *149*
Case, C.M., 91, *147*
Cheever, D.S., 2, *147*
Church, G.D., 25, *147*
Clements, D.H., 43, *149*
Coburn, P., 7, *148*
Collis, B., 7, 96, *148*

D

Daiute, C., 44, *148*
Dembrowski, F.L., *148*

F

Finkel, L., 72, *148*
Fisher, G., 72, *148*
Forcier, R.C., 7, *150*
Forman, K., 22, *148*
Friel, S., 7, *149*

G

Glossbrenner, A., 38, *148*
Goldenberg, E.P., 48, *148*
Goodson, B., 49, 52, *148*, *149*
Gould, S., 78, *148*
Gras, A., 48, *147*
Greensberg, H.M., 2, *149*
Guilbeau, J.J., 48, *148*
Gustafson, T.J., 2, *148*

H

Hai, D.M., 91, *148*
Hannifin, M.J., 66, *148*
Hertz, R., 44, *148*
Hill, F., 72, *148*
Hoover, T., 78, *148*
Hovey, K., 47, *150*
Hovey, L., 47, *150*
Hughes, B., 17, *149*
Hunter, B., 44, *148*

J

Jamison, D., 48, *148*

K

Kacanek, P., 35, *148*
Kauffman, D., 22, *150*
Kearsley, G., 66, 99, 116, 119, *148,*
    149, 150
Krahn, K., 17, *149*
Kulick, J.A., 48, *149*

L

Land, M., 7, *150*
Lathrop, A, 49, *149*
Lawler, R., 119, *149*
LeCesne, T., 44, *150*
Lindahl, R.A., 78, *147*

M

Miller, H., 2, *149*
Miller, M., 7, *149*

N

Niemiec, R., 48, *149*

P

Palmer, J., 43, *150*
Papert, S., 50, *149*
Peck, K., 66, *148*
Pennington, J.R., 31, *149*
Perelman, L., 111, *149*
Pogrow, S., 25, 85, *149*

R

Radin, S., 2, *149*
Riesdesel, C.A., 43, *149*
Roberts, N., 7, 47, *149*

Roblyer, M.D., 48, *149*
Russell, S., 48, *148*

S

Shneiderman, B., 116, *150*
Smith, R., 22, *150*
Snyder, T., 43, *150*
Stronge, J.H., 17, *150*

T

Thorman, J., 48, *147*
Trollip, S., 66, *147*
Turban, E., 25, *150*
Turner, J.H., 17, *150*
Turner, S., 7, *150*

W

Wagner, L., 99, *150*
Walberg, H., 48, *149*
Watt, D., 50, *150*
Watt, M., 50, *150*
White, G.T., 48, *150*
Williams, F., *150*
Williams, G.W., 48, *149*
Williams, R.C., 22, 85, *147*
Williams, V., *150*
Williams, W.L., 44, *150*
Willis, J., 47, *150*
Wresch, W., 44, *150*
Wright, E., 7, *150*

Y

Yazdani, M., 119, *149*

Subject Index

A
Absenteeism, 15
Air conditioning, 73
Authoring systems, 65

B
Backups, 31, 34
Bid requests, 88
Budgets, 13, 81, 102
Bulletin boards, 12
Bus routing, 24
Buying software, 25

C
Capital assets, 14
Computer
  benefits of, 4, 16, 17, 25
  competencies, 5
  conferencing, 37
  coordinator, 73
  district level, 14, 22
  goals for, 86–87
  instructional applications, 7
  instructional effectiveness, 46–48
  literacy, 1
  location of, 71–72
  maintenance, 107
  types of, 56
  usage data, 94
  viruses, 79
CD-ROM, 50, 67
Consultants, 75

Copyright infringement, 65, 69
Curriculum integration, 48
Cut & paste, 31

D
DOS, 62

E
Editing, 29
Electronic mail, 37, 119
Ergonomics, 57
Equal access, 72, 96
Expert systems, 118
Extensibility, 64

F
Facilities, 73
Formating, 29

G
Graphics Tablet, 59
Graphing, 36

H
Hacking, 79
Handicapped, 44, 60

I
IEPs, 20
Individualized instruction, 48, 119
Integrated databases, 20

L
Library specialist, 74
LOGO, 49

M
Mail merge, 31
Mouse, 59
Music, 51

N
Networking, 22, 41, 111–114, 122

O
OCR, 59
Online databases, 38
Optical scanning, 15, 59

P
Privacy, 21, 95
Productivity, 1–2, 11, 29
Programming, 49
Project Management, 91

R
Relational databases, 33
Reports, 13, 15, 18, 32
Report cards, 16

S
SAT preparation, 47
School management, 11
Screen resolution, 57
Security, 22, 33, 78–79
Software selection, 63–66
Software updates, 80
Speech input/output, 51, 59
Special education, 48
Storage, 73
Student databases, 20
Student preferences, 17
Student management software, 52

T
Teacher involvement, 76–77
Telecommunications programs, 38
Testing, 18
Touch input, 59
Troubleshooting, 80

U
UNIX, 62

V
Videodiscs, 50

W
Windowing, 57

Leadership in the Information Age
A simulation program for the IBM PC and PS/2

Leadership in the Information Age lets you experience the typical decisions that administrators face about the use of computers in schools. The program presents a series of events over the course of the year that you must deal with. Each screen provides a new challenge or opportunity for you to practice your decision-making skills. Your success in handling these events determines teacher and parent satisfaction, student behavior, and your own career advancement and recognition.

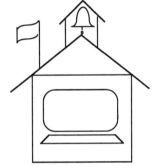

Since the events are randomly selected, you get a different set of situations each time you run the program. You can practice until you really understand the impact of different strategies and approaches. In addition, the program includes an editor that lets you change or add events and outcomes. Make up your own scenarios and results!

Not only is this program ideal for personal practice but it is useful for in-service training and class exercises.

Note: **Leadership in the Information Age** is a product of Park Row Inc., not Ablex. Please direct all inquiries to the address/phone number below.

- -

Yes, I want to try a copy of **Leadership in the Information Age.**
Please specify: __ 5 $1/4$" disk   __ 3 $1/2$" disk
☐ Check or purchase order for $49.95 plus $2.50 shipping is enclosed (CA add $3.25 sales tax).
☐ Charge my credit card $49.95 plus $4.50 shipping and handling (CA add $3.25 sales tax):
    __ MasterCard   __ VISA   Card # _ _ _ _ _ _ _ _ _ _ _ _ _ _ _   Expiry date: _ _ / _ _

Name _____
Address _____
_____
_____
Phone ( ) _____

Send to: Park Row Inc., 4640 Jewell St., #232, San Diego, CA 92109 or call (619) 581-6778